Women of Maize

Indigenous Women and the Zapatista Rebellion
Guiomar Rovira

Translated by Anna Keene

© Guiomar Rovira
First published as *Mujeres de Maíz: la voz de las indígenas de Chiapas y la rebelión Zapatista*, Editorial Era, Mexico

First published in the UK in 2000 by the Latin America Bureau, 1 Amwell Street, London EC1R 1UL

The Latin America Bureau is an independent research and publishing organisation. It works to broaden public understanding of issues of human rights and social and economic justice in Latin America and the Caribbean.

ISBN: 1 899365 30 3

Introduction © Dan Lewenstein
Translator: Anna Keene
Cover image: Fiona MacIntosh
Cover designer: Andy Dark
Print: Russell Press, Nottingham

Contents

The Zapatista uprising: the story so far... 1

Chapter 1   Settling the forest 16

Chapter 2   Dawn in the Zapatista forest 38

Chapter 3   Of love, marriage, children and war 44

Chapter 4   The women organise and
               become politically aware 66

Chapter 5   The Zapatista support base 96

Chapter 6   Everyday life in Los Altos de Chiapas 111

Chapter 7   Tzeltal women in the forest 137

Chapter 8   The Indigenous Clandestine
               Revolutionary Committee 148

Chapter 9   The dialogue on indigenous women 164

Chapter 10   Our hearts are set free 174

Glossary   180
Facts and Figures 182
Further Reading 183
Zapatista Timeline 184

Chiapas

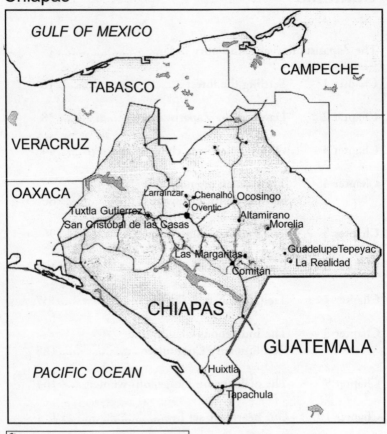

The Zapatista uprising: the story so far...

'I began, out of conscience, to fight in favour of the poor, since it is not right that they keep killing the children... When the enemy came, I felt brave, I wanted to kill someone, to shout with anger and hit them so that they would be humiliated as we have been humiliated for so long'.
Captain Laura, Zapatista National Liberation Army.

'What has come is something we never dreamed would happen...'
Subcomandante Marcos.

First impressions
On the 1st of January 1994, the Zapatista National Liberation Army (*Ejército Zapatista de Liberación Nacional*, EZLN) seized the city of San Cristóbal de las Casas and six other towns in the south-east Mexican state of Chiapas. The indigenous guerrillas, many with faces obscured by balaclavas, declared war to end the 70-year dictatorship of the Institutional Revolutionary Party (*Partido Revolucionario Institucional*, PRI), to stop 'dying from hunger and curable diseases', to halt the 'undeclared genocidal war' against the indigenous communities, and to achieve 'work, land, housing, food, health care, education, independence, freedom, democracy, justice and peace'.

Mexico and the world were shocked and intrigued by what had happened. Revolutions were considered outmoded in the new world order established by the West's victory in the Cold War. The insurrection occurred on the very day that Mexico entered the North American Free Trade Agreement (NAFTA), its supposed ticket to First World prosperity. Calling NAFTA a 'death certificate for the indigenous peoples', the EZLN left the image of a modernising Mexico in tatters. The world was reminded of the existence of Chiapas, one of Mexico's poorest states, where indigenous people have a life expectancy of only 44 years, 75% are malnourished and 30% of children do not attend school.

At the same time, these new Zapatistas challenged many preconceptions about the dogmatic and authoritarian nature of armed revolutionaries. The attitude of their apparent leader, described by one commentator as 'self-deprecating', surprised the reporters crowding around him in the central square of San Cristóbal. His orders came from the Clandestine Indigenous Revolutionary Committee, he explained, a democratic body in which six indigenous peoples, the Tzotzil, Tzeltal, Chol, Tojolabal, Mam and Zoque, are represented. He was one of only three non-indigenous 'ladinos' in what was essentially an indigenous ethnic movement. He was only a subcomandante; indeed, the capture of San Cristóbal had been directed by a woman, Major Ana Maria.

Together with Subcomandante Marcos' words, visual images of the insurgents were soon flashing around the globe. One striking feature of these pictures was the great number of women among the rebel soldiers; indeed, one third of the insurgent army are women, and many hold commanding positions. 'And women are in this movement voluntarily?' asked one disconcerted reporter on that first day. These physically small women, who had emerged from their villages beyond the pale of modern life, discarding 'exotic' traditional dress in favour of military uniforms and guns, abandoning their role as mothers and obedient workers to engage in combat and give orders, were something quite new and disconcerting, alien to familiar concepts of a 'revolutionary'.

A community in arms

How had this ragged army of largely illiterate peasants, many of them women or boys as young as fourteen, dealt such a blow to the credibility not only of the Mexican regime, but of the whole project of modern capitalist globalisation? The government immediately suggested sinister plots: the rebels were linked to drug traffickers, were armed and trained by foreigners. Yet it soon became clear that the secret of the EZLN's success was its deep, organic links to the indigenous communities of eastern Chiapas. It was this close relationship which had allowed thousands of guerrillas to move into Chiapas' cities, without alerting the Army, whose base at Rancho Nuevo lay only twelve kilometres from San Cristóbal.

Rather than an isolated band of revolutionaries, like the Mexican guerrillas of the seventies, who aimed to knock revolutionary consciousness into the heads of the masses through dramatic armed actions, the EZLN was the armed expression of an entire community in revolt. Though the EZLN can be traced back to a guerrilla nucleus which went into the mountains in 1983, this group spent eleven years working alongside the indigenous communities and developing its relationship with them before any armed action was taken. The guerrillas were forced to learn from indigenous people, to alter their slogans, conceptions and strategies to respond to the communities' needs. Slowly they had fused with the indigenous population, and the EZLN was born as the army of these communities. The declaration of war was a collective decision of the population.

If we understand the Zapatista uprising as a revolt of indigenous communities, against their exploitation and repression by external forces, the EZLN's lineage can be traced back far beyond 1983, down a very long line of indigenous rebellions. The EZLN has made this point explicitly, claiming in the first sentence of its Declaration of War, to be 'a product of five hundred years of struggle'.

Indigenous rebellion

The Spanish Conquest signified a dramatic drop in the living conditions of the people of Chiapas. The Spanish demanded exorbitant levels of tribute from a population which was being decimated by the epidemics that arrived with the conquerors. The 1712 Tzeltal rebellion is one good example of Chiapan peasants' struggle against colonial domination. Like the Zapatista rising, and many other peasant revolts, it involved a combination of outside influence and collective indigenous action, and a mix of economic and political preoccupations.

Historians have connected the 1712 rebellion to the fall in Chiapas' population due to epidemics at the end of the seventeenth century, which increased the tax burden on those who remained. However, the first signs of discontent came in 1708, when Tzeltals began to flock to the sermons of a wandering hermit, who was removed by the authorities and returned to even greater acclaim, before being recaptured and dying in the Crown's custody. Then in 1712, when a young girl declared she had seen the Virgin, the Tzeltals erected a shrine and demanded that the Church recognise its legitimacy. Instead, Dominican friars attempted to destroy the shrine, leading the Tzeltal elders to declare that they would no longer obey God or the King, and would kill all priests and Spaniards. The rising of six thousand Tzeltals was bloodily crushed in two months.

Like the Tzeltals of 1712, the Zapatistas of 1994 fight the economic and political impositions of the state and land-owners. They protest against the violent repression meted out by an alliance of the landlords' paramilitary 'white guards' and state security forces, who have excluded them from the most fertile lands, while demanding loyalty to the ruling party. In particular, the accelerated exploitation of Chiapas' great natural resources, which has taken place since the late 1960s, caused tremendous disruption to indigenous life. Proposals for 'development' in Chiapas have often seen the local population merely as an obstacle. Digging for oil and natural gas, the building of hydro-electric dams, the exploitation of the jungle by logging companies, have forced thousands to uproot themselves and migrate, often to less fertile lands.

Revolution within the revolution

Yet it would be wrong to conclude that this is a conservative rebellion, aiming to return to some hey-day of traditional indigenous village life. The startling images of indigenous women in arms are a clue to one important sense in which the EZLN is anti-traditional: the transformation of the lives of Zapatista women in the course of the revolt. Within the ranks of the indigenous guerrillas, a veritable revolution has occurred: indigenous women have won the right to marry whomever they want and divorce at will, to use contraception, to become literate and learn Spanish, and even to command male insurgents, while chores such as cooking are shared by both sexes. The flow of young women into the guerrilla, many taking up arms to avoid being forced into marriage, represents a series of individual revolts against the patriarchal status quo, and has been vital to the EZLN's success.

The EZLN's struggle is not only to liberate indigenous communities, but also to transform them. Thus it has fought to transfer the relative sexual equality of the insurgent army to the communities which provide its popular base, where gender relations still largely follow traditional patterns. 'The Women's Revolutionary Law', the first in a list of 'revolutionary laws' which were agreed by the Clandestine Indigenous Revolutionary Committee and published on the day of the uprising, has been key in this aspect of the Zapatista struggle. This decree, which was developed through a long process of consultation among indigenous women, seeks to alter traditional patriarchal domination, by outlawing rape, domestic violence and forced marriages, and establishing women's right to education, to work, to hold positions of authority, and to determine the number of children they will have.

The Zapatista attitude to tradition is thus a complex one. They have fervently opposed the government's suggestion that indigenous communities should be governed according to 'tradition and custom', not only because of their concern with the oppression of indigenous women, but because traditional community hierarchies have been used by the ruling Institutional Revolutionary Party as a channel to impose its domination. Traditional leaders were granted favours in return for their affiliation to the PRI, allowing indigenous villages to be integrated into the network of clientelistic relationships which provided the ruling party's social base. Rather than a return to traditional ways, the EZLN demands that communities have the right to determine their own rules collectively, to select the traditions they want to keep or to reject.

Revolt of identities

Instead of championing either 'tradition' or 'progress', the key ideological concept of the new Zapatista movement is 'autonomy'. The EZLN demands autonomy for indigenous communities in relation to the Mexican state and landlords, and also for groups and individuals within the communities themselves. It would be ludicrous to attempt to convert the slogan of 'autonomy' into some new all-embracing doctrine. However, the term is used by the EZLN as a way to shift power from the centre to marginalised sectors, and to recognise the coexistence of multiple identities in each state, community and individual human being.

The EZLN's sophisticated understanding of the complex nature of identity sets it apart from many ethnic movements. In ethnic conflicts in the Balkans, Rwanda and elsewhere, ethnicity has been elevated into an exclusive determinant of identity, requiring the exclusion or domination of those outside the favoured group. Other aspects of identity, such as gender or sexuality, and the multi-faceted nature of national and ethnic identity, have been sidelined. Such movements have commonly involved tremendous brutality towards women, valued only as reproducers of the 'correct' genetic material.

In contrast, the EZLN's discourse deals with identity on many different levels. Its members, from six different ethnic groups, unite as 'indigenous people' while respecting the diversity within that formula. At the same time they describe themselves as Mexican patriots, concerned to prevent the exploitation of Mexico by richer nations and to co-operate in the construction of a democratic state. Marcos considers this anti-imperialist nationalism to be a major impulse behind the indigenous peoples' declaration of war, and ridicules those intellectuals who believe that 'this type of consciousness is not possible in an indigenous person.' Finally, they declare their affiliation to a movement of 'humanity' against the dehumanising effects of neoliberal globalisation. While struggling for localised changes, the Zapatistas have unfurled a banner which aims to unite a far broader constituency: the construction, according to their slogan, of a 'world which has room for many worlds.'

Mexico in Chiapas

It is self-evident that the EZLN's attitude towards women has not emerged 'naturally' from the unadulterated experience of indigenous communities. Like every major indigenous revolt, the EZLN is the product of interaction between local indigenous reality and broader, national and international tendencies and ideas; even the 1712 Tzeltal rebellion took place under the banner of a Catholic Virgin. In recent years, the increasing integration of Chiapas into the world market has made the connections between Chiapas' peasants' concerns and national and international issues particularly clear.

The 1970s oil boom led many Chiapan peasants to leave the land to work in oil and related industries. When the oil bubble burst in the early eighties, many returned to their villages, having learnt Spanish as well as some basic lessons about the advantages and shortcomings of capitalist industrialisation. These bilingual people formed some of the initial links between the guerrilla and the communities. Women tended to stay within the communities and, like the outstanding female Zapatista leader, Comandante Ramona, to remain monolingual. Yet the changes in Chiapas' economy also altered their horizons: Zapatista women have demanded not only land, but also the right to be truck-drivers.

The EZLN cannot possibly be understood divorced from Mexican history or from international economic circumstances. The movement's very name derives from Emiliano Zapata, a revolutionary peasant leader from Morelos in central Mexico, who had no direct connection to Chiapas. When the wealthy liberal, Madero, declared a revolution against the dictator Porfirio Díaz in 1910, Zapata was chosen by the peasants of Morelos to lead them in support of the insurrection. Much like today's Zapatistas, Zapata's Liberation Army of the South was formed by the region's peasant communities to fight for 'land and freedom'. It established an egalitarian peasant republic in Morelos, its demands going far beyond Madero's call for formal democracy, and bringing it into conflict with the 'official' revolutionary forces, the Constitutionalists. Zapata's heroism and incorruptibility, and his final betrayal and

7

martyrdom at the hands of the victorious Constitutionalists, converted him into a powerful symbol of peasant dignity in the national psyche.

Yet Zapata's name did not become popular in Chiapas until much later, when it was carried there by agrarian activists from other regions of Mexico. At the time, the revolution was kept out of Chiapas by the paramilitary bands of local landlords. Land ownership continued to be dominated by massive estates, fincas, in which indigenous peasants were treated as virtual slaves, and the women considered the sexual property of the estate owner.

Post-revolutionary land reform

The land reform carried out by post-revolutionary governments did, however, reach Chiapas, in the 1930s and 1940s. Thousands of hectares of land were redistributed in the form of *ejidos*, to be farmed collectively by peasant communities. Land reform was inspired by the revolutionary Constitution of 1917, and formed the basis for the state-led development strategy of the ruling group, which in the 1940s was to become the Institutional Revolutionary Party. Aside from its economic benefits, land reform bound peasants to the ruling party; such populist policies allowed the PRI to develop clientelistic networks throughout Mexico, distributing benefits in return for political loyalty.

Yet the post-revolutionary regime had come to power through the destruction of Zapata's radical agrarianism. Its land reform programme was limited, leaving the power of the great landlords intact. When the fincas, or haciendas, were broken up, landlords were allowed to select the best part of each estate to keep for themselves, ensuring them control over vital resources such as irrigation. It was not sufficient for Chiapas' peasants to have land, without the means to cultivate it effectively. Moreover, rapid population growth meant that the redistributed land soon became insufficient for peasants' needs.

However, the PRI maintained the support, or at least passivity, of indigenous communities, through its 'indigenist' policies. The National Indigenist Institute (*Instituto Nacional de Indigenismo*, INI) provided funds to indigenous communities in return for their loyalty to the ruling party. Indigenous peoples were thus brought into Mexico's 'corporatist' political system, which sought to tie different social actors to the state, through the integration of traditional village hierarchies into the PRI's structures.

Crisis of Mexican corporatism

By the 1970s, however, Mexican corporatism had entered into a prolonged crisis, both in Chiapas and nationally. The arrival of petro-dollars in Chiapas led to increased social differentiation, tending to break up community ties and destabilise established paternalistic relationships. Whereas previously those in authority required a degree of popular support, monetary power now made this less crucial. Landlords and politicians increasingly enforced their will through financial muscle, hiring paramilitary goons to suppress peasants' demands for land.

These developments mirrored a process in Mexican society as a whole, which was encapsulated by the government's massacre of hundreds of protesting students in Mexico City in October 1968. 1968 gave birth to a generation of political militants, disillusioned with the regime and determined to transform Mexican society. Some of this politicised generation went to Chiapas, where they coincided with the development of Liberation theology in the ranks of the Catholic priesthood. Radical priests preached the need for the poor to educate themselves and to struggle for a better life on earth, while political groups helped the peasants to organise. Both found a receptive audience in Chiapas, leading to the development of a variety of indigenous organisations which campaigned for land reform, cheap credit and assistance in marketing crops.

Such campaigns also began to open up the vistas of indigenous women. The movement towards education of women had been initiated by Protestant evangelists in search of converts, who began to win indigenous adherents in the 1970s. Later, feminist ideas, which formed part of the 1968 flowering of radicalism, gradually filtered down to Chiapas. By the 1980s various women's organisations had been established in the region.

Neoliberalism

In the early 1980s, pressure from international financial institutions led the Mexican government to abandon its historic populism and adopt orthodox neoliberal economic policies, including tough austerity measures, massive privatisation and the opening up of Mexican markets to foreign capital. While a handful became millionaires (Carlos Slim, a close friend of former president Salinas, became the fifth richest man in the world in 1997), the consequence for most Mexicans was a drastic fall in living standards. For Chiapas peasants this meant the withdrawal of some government subsidies, resulting in the collapse of coffee prices (one of Chiapas' main crops) in 1989. More critically, in 1992 President Salinas announced the reform of Article 27 of the Constitution, enshrining land reform, which was now brought to a halt, putting a damper on peasants' hopes of a better future.

Repression was also stepped up by the new governor, Patrocinio Gonzalez, who took office in 1988. In its formative stages, the EZLN was regarded as a self-defence organisation by the communities, serving to repel the attacks of landlords and security forces. Yet the population became increasingly disillusioned with peaceful campaigning organisations, which were often bought off by the authorities, their leaders being converted into distributors of government patronage which had been won through campaigns. The infamous electoral fraud of 1988, in which the PRI claimed victory after declaring that the computer system had crashed, and later burnt the ballot papers before they could be examined, appeared to shut off the electoral road to change. Then, the 1992 reform of Article 27 meant that legal acquisition of lands would no longer be possible, leaving thousands of peasants with unresolved claims. It was at this time that a mass influx into the EZLN occurred in eastern Chiapas as peasants deserted the peaceful campaigning organisations, concluding that arms were the only realistic way forward.

The world meets Chiapas

The growth of EZLN took place at a time when revolutionary organisations were on the retreat across Latin America and the world: the Nicaraguan Sandinistas had been voted out of power, and the FMLN of El Salvador had disarmed. As Marcos commented, 'When everything internationally was saying no to armed struggle, indigenous peasants in Chiapas were saying yes, yes, yes.' However, despite the surprise caused by the 1994 uprising, many of the issues raised by the EZLN found an immediate echo throughout Mexico and beyond its borders. The Zapatistas tapped into national and international opposition to neoliberal economics, and appeared to offer a new way to drive forward democratic reform, which had been stalled by the 1988 fraud. Zapatista literature stressed democratic demands, calling for a transitional government to oversee the 1994 elections, to prevent a new fraud. This was a key issue for the EZLN, who perceive the PRI dominance as underpinning the hierarchical and oppressive social structure of Chiapas.

The popular support which the EZLN elicited nationally was of great importance. The superior force of the Mexican Army soon obliged the insurgents to retreat, as 12,000 troops and sophisticated military equipment was moved into the area. But the pressure of public opinion and international media attention led the regime to hold back, rather than pursuing the guerrillas into the jungle to liquidate them. On 12 January a massive demonstration took place in Mexico City, demanding that the government respond with negotiation rather than repression, and President Salinas declared a unilateral cease-fire on the same day.

Thus the uprising was converted into a long stand-off, with EZLN-government talks periodically broken off and then reopened, and each side manoeuvring for advantage while avoiding a return to all-out conflict. Since 1994, the government has fought a clandestine, 'low-intensity war' against the Zapatista base communities, systematically arming and training paramilitary groups such as 'Red Mask' and 'Peace and Justice', with the objective of breaking the communities' loyalty to the EZLN through terror. Amongst other atrocities, these groups were responsible for the massacre of 45 indigenous people at Acteal in December 1997.

In contrast, the EZLN's principal weapons have been political, aiming to rally national opinion behind them: communiqués, conferences, demonstrations and popular ballots to 'consult' with Mexican society. Their initial hope, of detonating a democratic transition in Mexico, was severely set back by the PRI's 1994 electoral victory, which, while certainly cleaner than 1988, was undoubtedly aided by clientelistic practices such as the distribution of patronage to loyal areas through Salinas' 'Solidarity' committees.

The 1995 talks shifted the terrain of debate to questions of indigenous autonomy. The EZLN's proposals aimed to break down the PRI's domination of communities and to alleviate repression, by permitting indigenous communities their own forms of independent political and judicial administration. Yet the San Andres agreement, signed by both sides in February 1996, was later repudiated by the government, whom Marcos accused of using the negotiations only to gain time for the training of paramilitary forces. President Zedillo (who replaced Salinas in 1994) now rejected clauses allowing indigenous zones to define their own boundaries for municipal government, and to administer justice without outside interference.

The EZLN has so far been unable to break the negotiations deadlock; its great achievement has been to survive. The Zapatistas have maintained their communities, in the face of constant harassment from the military and paramilitary forces, and the cutting off of state support, and turned them into a model of egalitarian and sustainable development. They have established clinics, taking advantage of traditional indigenous medical knowledge, set up schools and cultivated organic crops for sale abroad. They have compensated for their isolation by building strong networks with sympathetic NGOs from around the world. In managing to do all this they have offered an alternative to the neoliberal model of development.

Meanwhile, the Mexican political system has undergone a process of change, with the disintegration of the PRI's one-party regime. The process, which culminated in the victory of the opposition National Action Party (*Partido de Acción Nacional*, PAN) candidate, Vicente Fox, in the 2000 presidential elections, was certainly helped on its way by the EZLN's 1994 alarm call. The PRI's political bankruptcy was exposed by its inability to resolve the crisis in Chiapas; during the campaign Fox boasted that he would bring the conflict to an end in 'fifteen minutes'.

What is far less clear is whether this change will be a favourable one for the EZLN and the indigenous communities. The PAN is the inheritor of the traditions of Mexican conservatism, a political sector which for 70 years was marginalised due to its opposition to the basic rights won by Mexican workers and peasants during the Revolution, but has now re-emerged, supported by the new business elite (Fox himself is a wealthy businessman) and blending 'back-to-basics' Catholic morality with orthodox neoliberal economics. The place accorded to indigenous people in this new 'democratic' Mexico is as yet unclear, but the EZLN's continued presence at least ensures it will feature on the political agenda.

Ramona In Mexico City

The joke going around at the time was that were the Zapatistas to march on Mexico City, as they had originally declared they would, they would be wiped out by the city's infamous smog. Yet in February 1997 the first EZLN leader did arrive in Mexico's metropolis. The spectacle was somewhat different from 83 years before, when the peasant armies of Zapata and Pancho Villa had seized the city. The EZLN Comandante arrived without troops or weapons, to speak to the people of Mexico City; moreover, she was a

13

woman. The disconcerting image of Comandante Ramona, indigenous woman and revolutionary leader, who addressed the crowds through an interpreter due to her lack of Spanish, spoke volumes about the deeply radical nature of the Zapatista project. This new image of revolutionary woman contrasted sharply with the 'Adelitas' of the 1910 Revolution, camp-followers who prepared food for the male fighters and were generally stereotyped as submissive wives or wanton whores.

Ramona's visit was one example of the way that this essentially local movement has been able to use radical ideas and innovative images to invade the territory of national and even international politics. At the time of publication, over six years since the indigenous peoples of Chiapas announced their existence to the world, the 'spectre' of the EZLN continues to haunt the Mexican state. The Zapatistas were a major inspiration for the explosive student movement of 1999, which led to the closure for over a year of Latin America's largest university, the National Autonomous University of Mexico (UNAM). Their example has also given rise to new armed guerrilla groups in other areas of the country, such as the Popular Revolutionary Army (*Ejército Popular Revolucionario*, EPR).

Whatever the future holds, the Zapatista uprising stands as a testament to the possibility for social change which exists within human beings. The Zapatistas have challenged claims by neoliberal politicians that they represent the will of all Mexicans. They have powerfully asserted the continued existence and pride of indigenous communities. Moreover, they have altered the conceptions, both of society at large and of indigenous women themselves, of what the lives of indigenous women can aspire to.

In this book Guiomar Rovira has sought to preserve this rich, humanising experience by recording the testimony of indigenous women both in the guerrilla army and in the Zapatista base communities. Here, Zapatista women explain their cause in their own words. These women are political fighters, who consciously demand our attention, sympathy and solidarity. Yet their political message is constantly intertwined with personal experience, and their words reveal more than could the observations of any outsider about the daily reality of indigenous women. Most exciting of all are the insights they provide into the deep psychological implications of the shift in power relations, in favour of indigenous people in general and of indigenous women in particular, which the Zapatista rebellion brought about.

Dan Lewenstein
August 2000

Chapter 1

Settling the forest

When the first four families arrived in Guadalupe Tepeyac, a hamlet deep inside the Lacandon jungle, it was just forest. It was an inhospitable place for the Tojolabal settlers, who, fed up of working as farm hands, had finally fled the *fincas*. Of the first founders only a few women remain, and they are old now.

It was the women who suffered most when, on 10 February 1995 more than half a century after they colonised this corner of forest, they had to flee their community, escaping over the mountains. The Mexican Army had invaded the area, using hundreds of soldiers in helicopters. The people of Guadalupe decided to seek shelter in a hospital run by the International Red Cross, but the soldiers came after them anyway.

All the little houses and huts were searched extensively. The Guadalupanos, including the old women, abandoned the village. With nothing but the clothes they had on, they began an exodus into the mountains, running away from the 'social work' and the 'restoration of the rule of law' brought by the army.

Even hundred-year-old Doña Herminia, slender as a willow, wrinkled and worn, made the journey. Her almost blue eyes are surprisingly lively. She seems childlike, girlish. She doesn't have a tooth left, her legs are sticks, just bones. Her dark Tojolabal skin has furrows like the earth. They had to carry her, there was no way she could walk for three days and nights, so her sons made a makeshift stretcher out of branches.

It was not by chance that we interviewed Doña Herminia. We had managed to gain access to the Guadalupanos' hiding place, only two weeks after they fled their village. They were precariously settled in a corner of the Lacandon forest. We were about to leave when a man approached us:

16

- Have you spoken to Doña Herminia?
- Who is Doña Herminia?
- The wisest woman in the village, he replied.

He pointed to one of the huts. In the darkness inside we saw a woman lying on a bed made of wooden boards. She had a scarf tied around her head and wore a flowered dress. Her legs were covered by a Guatemalan blanket. Doña Herminia was sitting up sipping coffee from a bowl. Mother, grandmother, great-grandmother, great-great-grandmother, more than a century old, this woman regarded us with curiosity. Then she greeted us warmly, extending her bony hand. Smoothing out the blanket and straightening her hair, she sighed. That sigh and piercing gaze introduced what she had to say. She was fine, but so far away from home!

- We are sad here. They carried me, I can't walk, my legs hurt too much. Dear God, how we are suffering. The small children, all of them, with hardly any *tortillas* to eat.

In the same hut where Doña Herminia sits are another ten families. There is insufficient space for the men, who spend the night under the stars. One of Herminia's daughters, Zoraida, in her eighties already, seemed to be more upset than her mother. She couldn't hold back her tears when she told us what leaving the village meant to her. She cried remembering how 'they were carrying my mother, my poor mother'. Despite her age Zoraida walked the four days like everyone else until they reached a safer place. Extremely thin and tall, Zoraida looks strong and fit. She is wearing a sky-blue dress that she has to 'wash and wear again', because she couldn't take anything with her when they fled. Her voice is melodic and sweet and she worries a lot for the little ones. The first time we visited her in that forest shelter, Zoraida was worrying because she had no clothes for her grandchildren. She couldn't come to terms with her fate. Along with one of her *comadres* (a friend) Doña Chole, she told us why she was so tired of suffering.

Starting life in Guadalupe Tepeyac

And that's how we heard their history and how they came to live in Guadalupe Tepeyac. Chole began:

- I am one of the original founders of Guadalupe, along with another *comadre*. We were among the first to arrive. I left a small hut in Santa Isabel. My late husband said: 'there's not enough for us to eat here. The children are growing, but where will they work? I'll find a place'. I replied: 'wherever you go, I'll follow'. Why would I stay alone with the children?

Zoraida took up the tale:

- I came with my first children, then others were born here. One child was born just outside the village. The rest of them were born in Guadalupe Tepeyac. We came to the forest because we thought there would be good land for maize and we would be able to grow our food, so our husbands decided to go and look for a little plot of land. We were not sure whether to come because we were told it was very hot and that it would be hard to get used to it. But my husband said, 'No, my girl, let's go because here there is no future for our children'. That's why we came to this bloody forest, and just look what's happening to us now.

The first settlers pitched their tents and began to work. They came from properties with masters, they were labourers. The indigenous people, landless *campesinos*, came to colonise the state lands of the Lacandon forest. Many of them, before setting out on this venture, got property deeds as *ejidos* for different bits of the forest. Others went straight to work the land while waiting for their legal papers to come through. Some arrived in Guadalupe Tepeyac with no deeds at all.

Zoraida recounts:

- I was born on a farm in El Porvenir, near La Petema. My parents lived under the rule of the master. They worked for him all week, they had only Sundays for themselves. In Guadalupe they made an *ejido* and four or five people settled on it. The family grew and so did Guadalupe. Later on, more settlers arrived, but they had trouble getting government authorisation. My uncle was shot for requesting land, that was forty-two years ago. They had begun to sort out the

18

deeds and had cleared a part of the mountain, to build houses, that was my uncle's only crime. They shot him but he didn't die. Two people went to jail for it. It was hard having the army around.

Doña Chole continues:

- It was difficult to build up the *ejido*. My husband was shot by the federal police because of a plot of land. There wasn't any way to sort it out, we didn't know why we were neglected and treated like animals. They broke in, firing shots. I told my children: 'Don't move, stay in bed'. We couldn't do anything. But I wasn't afraid and asked: 'show me your warrant. Why are you staring at us? What do you plan to do to us? They will know about this in the President's office'. They didn't even listen to me. They fired, and a shot hit him and he went to Las Margaritas. That's how it turned out. A *compadre* was locked up in jail for trying to get his plot. However, we finally got our land.

Somewhere in the forest, these old women keep alive their longing for their village invaded by soldiers, and recall their arrival to what they called Guadalupe:

- The men started to clear the forest. We worked to clear that piece of land, we hardly ate. We had no beans, coffee or salt, we had nothing. That's why I tell you: we went without so much that I don't want to suffer any more. It's the same now but worse.

- Many of the men got fevers and died, leaving us all widows. They were still in their prime but they got ill and there was nothing to cure them with. Just women, and children too small to help their parents. More people came, so we had some company, relatives who didn't have a place to live. We were dirt poor, all we had was each other. We had nothing, but we had land.

- When we became widows, we went to earn some money on the coffee harvest at the nearby farms. When they paid us we could get some clothes for the children. We were paid two *reales* per load. When we started here we really suffered, but we are still here.

Zoraida sheds more tears. As an EZLN communiqué says 'seventy thousand olive green reasons' keep her from going back to Guadalupe Tepeyac, considered a bastion of the insurgency. Zoraida, like everyone in her town, at no time questions the right of the Zapatista movement to rise up, she only asks for the army to leave.

19

She says the soldiers scare her, her daughters and great-grandchildren. She repeats over and over that they don't deserve to be tested again like when they first settled. They went through so much suffering:

- It's very dangerous nowadays and we are suffering all over again. We suffered when we came to the forest for a piece of land. We couldn't eat beans or maize or drink coffee, because the plants were too small, we had nothing. Not even clothes, just mended rags, washed and worn.

Who can imagine the conditions these women faced when they first came to the forest? They had to give birth alone, had to invent something to eat, carry the children, help their husbands exhausted by hard physical labour, watch their people die of disease, far from any medicine, far from the basic elements of their traditional world.

Men tamed the virgin land. The women had to start from scratch too, when so many things were lacking:

- Before, we couldn't even get soap, nothing. We would get the kids to help us, pounding an amolio leaf, a small pod like this, and wash the clothes with it in a bucket. We didn't have any money because the farms where we picked coffee paid us so little. But what could we do? We had to earn something, I had young sons and daughters, as did the other women. We all worked equally hard. Four of us came to settle down here. We really lamented our bad luck because we couldn't find anything when we came. We didn't have any kitchen utensils, just clay pots. We crushed glass to make our clay pots. There weren't any tools, just a machete we took from where we used to live under the master...

We started afresh in Tepeyac and we've already suffered enough. But since we all became widows it's been even worse. That's why we feel so bad.

Sitting in the open shelter where she sleeps, lying on the earth along with another forty refugees, Chole concludes:

- Our destiny was decided by God, that's for sure, because as human beings we are made to suffer in this world and if God himself suffered, then no wonder we do too...

Towards the Ahlan K inal

Indigenous migration into the forest was at its height from the 1940s until the 1970s. It is estimated that, by the 1990s, more than one hundred and fifty thousand people inhabit this area, now considered a 'conflict zone' and 'Zapatista territory.'

- Why did we decide to come here? Well, looking for a place where we could eat a little better. Truly our poverty hurt... because we had no land. If we had enough land, what would we be doing here, suffering like this?

- My in-laws were very sad when they saw me leaving with their daughter, to a destiny unknown to us all. My life was decided in an instant... On that same day I took a plane and flew to a place called Ahlan K'inal, at the end of the earth.

Colonisation began with the founding of two villages. This required working hard to create a community in order to face the initial difficulties and a hostile environment. The key to this process was determination and a struggle for life which has proved to be the seedbed of the EZLN. Different ethnic communities came together. Tzotziles married Tzeltales, Tzeltales married Tojolabales, Choles married Tzotziles. These couples communicated in the husband's dialect, which is why many women became bilingual. Many learnt Spanish because it was useful to sell the harvest, to defend their rights and campaign for their demands. The women, whether monolingual or bilingual, rarely spoke Spanish at home. It is not surprising that even if they understand it, they don't let on. The Tojolabal women, more used to dealing with *ladinos* in the farms and valleys of Comitán, are the ethnic group with the most Spanish-speaking women. They coexist with many *mestizos*, poor *campesinos* who also fled to the Lacandon forest.

In the forest they had to work together to succeed. Many of the men became polyglots and travellers. For many of the women, the forest also provided the chance to break out of the stifling discipline of their former lives.

In Nuevo Huixtón and Nuevo Matzam, researchers from the University of Chiapas collected the stories of Tzotzil and Tzeltal women who lived in these two enclaves of the Lacandona National

Reserve, in Las Margaritas municipality. They didn't come from the *fincas*, but from Los Altos de Chiapas, where the extreme poverty forced their husbands to hire themselves out to the land-owners as seasonal labourers.

The collected stories produced by the University, Skop Anzetik, *A History of Women in the Chiapas Forest*, tells of their experience:

- We didn't know if it was going to be better here. We were used to *tierra fría* (the cold lands, the highlands), and we didn't want to leave our home.

'I don't want to leave my mother', said some.

'No, I don't want to go, I'm afraid of the water they say is there'.

'I'm not going', we said.

But what could we women do, when the men had already decided we were going to the Reserva Nacional?

The women's subordinate position gave them no other option but to join in the venture.

'If you don't want to go, then stay here', said the husbands, but some of us women were dragged away, beaten. In fact only a few of us came of our own free will.

We were loaded down with things and those of us with bigger families had one child in our arms, another on our back and the older ones walking next to us. We went to San Cristóbal and there we took the truck to Comitán, at least that's the name we were told, because in fact we scarcely knew the places we passed on the way.

We bought a ticket and travelled until the end of the road, the truck didn't take us all the way. So we were left in the middle of the mountain, who knows what that place was called. But we remembered how long the journey felt; three, four, even five days hard walking ... we women fell back to the rear, almost getting lost. We were crying because we couldn't go any faster, with the mud coming up to our knees. The children sank right into it and we had to help them every step of the way. We felt like we were dying, our hearts tight in our chests from so much heat and thirst, and even the shade of the trees didn't help... it felt like the whole world was on fire....

We were even sadder when we reached the river, there we began to cry from fear when we saw how wide and green it was and we had never seen anything like it before. We thought we would die and the fish would eat us.

Many of us wanted to turn back, but it was too late so we covered our faces with our shawls or held on tight to our husbands or had a drink of alcohol, anything to give us courage and we made it across.

The majority of the indigenous women who came down out of the forest had never left their immediate surroundings before. All they knew of the world was their mountain village and at most the city of San Cristóbal de las Casas. The climate there is temperate to cold. But as they penetrated the forest, the temperature rose, the vegetation got denser, the air thickened. The journey into the forest was an odyssey for them and often a traumatic one at that, not only because of 'the many insects and mosquitoes and the snakes and other wild animals…'

Overnight these pioneer wives and daughters were removed from their customs, taken far away from relatives and neighbours and their familiar environment. Although some groups carried their saints into the jungle, the majority of the new communities had no temple or other place of worship. In addition, their traditional thick woollen skirts smothered them in this environment. There was neither sheep for wool to weave nor any of the herbs that they used for healing.

In the promised land, then, the women felt lost.

- 'I am not going to let you go back home', said the husbands. 'We are here to stay.' This made us women very sad. Many of us fell sick and nearly died of a broken heart.

- So that's how it was. We had to put up with all the suffering and even being far from our relatives, not knowing if our grandparents or parents or children were sick. We were not able to talk to them and they died without us.

- We are a long way away, we can't even see our sick ones. Only much later did we find out they had died and we didn't see them.

23

And the granddaughters became rebels too

Although they gained their freedom and in many cases land to cultivate, the indigenous people who went to the forest continued to live in conditions of abject scarcity. In the inaccessible corners of the Lacandon area there are no public services and the nearest hospital, school, shop or transport is a long way off.

Commandante Trinidad of the EZLN lives in Guadalupe Tepeyac. During the San Andrés Larraínzar dialogue in May 1995 she said:

- In the forest we no longer had a boss but we were just as poor as before, as we had nothing to sell. Our struggle emerged from that poverty because we weren't listened to; we were abandoned.

Trini is part of a generation which has given up its sons and daughters to the armed struggle. The insurgent troops are mostly young people, many of them born into the terrible poverty of the new forest communities.

Silvia is an EZLN captain. She is a Chol and eighteen years old. She was born in a small Lacandon village and her parents were among the first settlers. Silvia only has vague memories of her childhood but she does know that her vocation for struggle is rooted in her past.

- I have four brothers and sisters. I worked in the fields, I didn't go to school. In my community there was a school built out of mud and grass. The teachers turned up sometimes but just did a register of the pupils, they didn't teach. My *ejido* is very poor; there's nothing there. I used to help my mother because my family are very poor, no money, no nothing. If the kids get ill there's nowhere to go, no road to get out and no doctors anyway. You have to walk for eight hours carrying the sick person. They usually die. But it's not right that someone who just has a temperature or other curable illness has to die.

- The women have nothing. They do housework, fetch wood, go to work, make *tortillas*, prepare the food, help their husbands clear the maize fields, and look after the kids. Some, not all, take part in the meetings of the communities, those who can understand, that is. I knew that there was an armed organisation, the EZLN, a long time ago. Someone mentioned it to me, someone from elsewhere, not our

24

village. I began to think about the eleven points that the EZLN is fighting for. And that's why I am proud to have joined. No one comes just for the fun of it. We are exploited by the government, by the powerful.

The idea of armed struggle penetrated into the deepest forest ravines. Government repression and violence against indigenous people only highlighted further the only option available; understood in many cases as self-defence. Silvia experienced this herself.

- In my village we were not all with the EZLN and in 1990 we were betrayed. About five hundred armed federal agents searched the whole community and found weapons. We had some small organised groups, which is why they investigated us, because they wanted to know who the leader of the *ejido* was. Someone talked and told everything including names. They made arrests. Some people were able to hide but they took the leaders away and some did not reappear. Those that fled managed to make it here to this village but they were hunting for them in the mountains, shooting all over the place and killing. Some people I never saw again.

- Azucena, another rebel and I were taken to a safe house in San Cristóbal where the federal police couldn't find us. While I was working in a house in the city I thought long and hard about what to do. I asked to go to the mountain to take up arms. 'I know that it is a sacrifice but it is time to take sides and that's why I am here'. I haven't seen my family since 1989, they don't know where I am. The army are in control of the *ejido* now.

- I am proud to be here in the EZLN, because it's necessary. Also you learn here. At home you do nothing but work, preparing food and don't learn anything, so it's better to come here. We take up arms for the good of our people. Previously I didn't speak Spanish, only Chol, but they've taught me everything and now I'm doing quite well.

Together with Silvia, Azucena experienced the military invasion of their *ejido* which culminated in the razing and burning of the little straw huts in which they lived. From then on, despite her tender age, she was clear that she wanted to join the rebels.

- I didn't think too hard about it. I just came here and it all

25

happened quickly. I was in the militia just three days and then they sent me here. I think I am probably eighteen and I have been in the EZLN for three years. We are not fighting for money. We have taken up arms, which is not easy, but we are determined to do this for our people. Perhaps with weapons the government will understand us. I feel at ease with myself and besides there is no other way.

Elisa is another rebel captain, a Tzeltal by origin. She left one of the many new forest communities where the poverty was unbearable. She is twenty-three years old:

- I have been in the Zapatista Army for five years. I decided to join because I could see the situation of my people. Beforehand I didn't know that there were *compañeros* preparing for the struggle and to help the people. But when I found out, I went to the mountains, prepared to join the war and to join the EZLN. Of course nobody likes to become an insurgent but, given the situation, we all have to make an effort and put up with it so that the people get what they need. Because we have so often seen that people organise, go on marches, strikes and nothing ever gets solved, which is why it is better to take up arms. And to do that you have to be in the mountains, with all the suffering and problems, like your commanding officer saying you have to walk all night, putting up with the cold, tiredness and rain.

Death

Major Ana María, a twenty-nine year-old Tzotzil, replies to our question 'Aren't you afraid of death?':

- No, death means nothing to us. In the past we didn't really exist anyway, no one took any notice of us. There has been so much death in the communities from disease and hunger that we say it's as though we were always at war. As for those who have died, yes of course it pains us, but some have to give their lives for there to be justice and freedom in this country. We women are committed to this struggle and we are not afraid to die. It is more painful to see the children dying of curable diseases, measles, whooping cough, tetanus, cholera, illnesses that the government says no longer exist. I don't have any children but I have watched two little girls die in my arms. We couldn't do anything because the mother had already died and there was no food for them. Thousands of other children like them have died; it is not right. All during the time that we were carrying out struggle by peaceful means, without getting anywhere, many, very many, children died. Every time there was an illness it just cut a swathe through the community and they would have to build larger cemeteries. That is very painful and that's why we decided to do this.

(San Cristóbal Cathedral, 27 February 1994).

Another guerrilla girl, Maribel, twenty-six years old and a captain, says:

- Death appears practically overnight in the communities, with diarrhoea, vomiting, high temperatures. That's why we say being an insurgent or militia-woman is not difficult. The hardest thing is what the people suffer: injustice, no education, no food, which is harder because it is all day every day. Our life is hard; you have to run, jump, walk, fight, but it's not forever. The suffering of the community is constant.

Chapter 2

Dawn in the Zapatista forest

It's April 1994. Dawn is beginning to creep through the Chiapas forest. A wooden shed is surrounded by trees and shrubs while birds begin to sing inside the hundred year-old ceiba. It is just six o'clock in the morning and the world seems to be waking up from a long sleep, wiping the sleep from its eyes, opening them to the sunlight. Objects that were draped with night are becoming visible.

Birds and animals take over from silence and the green replaces darkness. A radio-cassette player is turned on inside the hut. A cumbia sounds clearly. 'I am happy, happy 'cos I'm in love...' and after that comes 'Ronalda, take off your miniskirt...' The sleeping inhabitants of the hut begin to stir. It is a cramped space, about four by four metres. Inside are makeshift board bunks, held in place with lianas and other ropes made from vegetation. Holsters, rifles, different kinds of weapons, hang from the walls or lie beside their owners. The floor is covered with boots, most of them old, torn and mended. In the darkness of the shed the voices of the youngsters getting up can be heard in laughter and complaint. Some of them are female. They've slept with their uniforms on, covered with a blanket. They put on their boots, hang their rifles on their shoulders and leave.

Lieutenant Lucio arrives. He's nineteen years old and handsome. He smiles, scratches his head, fixes his cap and goes into the next hut, the kitchen, made out of ill-fitting wooden boards with a blackened straw roof. Two young girls dressed in black and brown come out of the hut, carrying combs in their hands. Their long hair falls like obsidian over their uniforms. Rigoberta is wearing a coloured bead necklace, Consuelo wears long earrings. Talking all the while, they toss their hair forwards, comb it and plait it. Two little bobbles, red and orange like sweets, top their handiwork, which peeps out underneath their caps.

28

Captain Irma is sitting in front of the radio-communications set. Rigoberta and Consuelo stand to attention and salute her.

- Good morning, Captain.

Irma, listening to the voices on her radio, replies distractedly:

- Oh…good morning.

Irma is twenty-eight years old. She is slightly freckled, even though she is a Chol. Her eyes are black and sparkling. She is a Captain, a woman, but at the same time she is a child. Laughter, jokes and a love of life emanate from her.

She carries a submachine gun she 'recovered' from a member of the judicial police during the capture of Ocosingo. Later, she will tell how she enrolled in the EZLN because she had a brother who was a Zapatista:

- In our village, since the houses are very small and there are lots of children, I was going to be married off without my knowledge. So, when I found out, I preferred to leave instead. I didn't love that man, and I was too young.

In the kitchen, just a small dark shed where they cook with firewood, two uniformed boys make breakfast. Their rifles hang from the nail for the pots. They got up earlier than the rest, went to look for firewood and lit the fire. Then they brought water from the nearest source and put it to boil for the beans, coffee and rice. It's their shift in the kitchen today. Tasks are rotated at HQ and shared between men and women alike. Before they were Zapatista soldiers, when they lived in their parents' houses, they never saw a man near the fire making *tortillas*. Now, while seven rebel *compañeras* sleep, these boys cook breakfast for everyone.

Irma comments to me:

- In the villages it is the woman who does the housework, only women make *tortillas* and do the washing. Here is not like that, men work too, the *compañeros*, they also do the daily work at the HQ.

The Captain makes sure that the cooks have completed their tasks and asks what is going to be cooked for the evening and if there is going to be anything special like a tin of sardines. For the boys it is the most natural thing in the world to receive orders from her and even when they don't like cooking, they say that as soldiers they have

29

no choice but to follow orders. 'And that is only fair', adds Leonel.

Irma's partner is a rebel too, Major Rolando. Rolando told me that the most difficult thing for him since he joined the EZLN was learning how to cook beans.

- At the beginning it is very hard to live in the forest, you have to get used to the environment; but well, we were already used to the labour. The hardest thing for me was cooking. One day I burned the beans, imagine that, serving burnt beans to all the *compañeros*.

Rolando had to stay at headquarters until he learned how to cook beans. And he did. It is seven o'clock in the morning and it's time for breakfast. About fifteen rebels have emerged from the hut. Seven are women. They've put on their caps, washed their hands and faces and fixed up their hair. They come into the kitchen and take one of the prepared fifteen bowls. The dried *tortillas* are toasting on the fire and serve as spoons. Lieutenant Lucio serves coffee for everyone. This is what they eat: rice and beans. The portions are big enough but it's pretty monotonous. On some special days they get eggs or tuna or meat. Sometimes pasta is served instead of rice. That is as much as their diet varies, besides coffee or *atole*. 'Now we eat well, but when we are in the mountains... ay,' sighs a young lieutenant.

Life in the villages

Not far away from the encampment, in the nearest hamlet, from three o'clock in the morning many housewives are devoting their efforts to produce that round maize miracle, the *tortilla*, the basis of everything, their cosmology, their nutrition, the round piping-hot yellow miracle that calms hunger pangs and represents both the Mayan sun and woman's never-ending labour.

Major Ana María, from Los Altos de Chiapas, described the working day of an indigenous woman:

- She doesn't stop during the whole day. The *campesino* woman gets up in the early hours of the morning to make the *pozol* and the food for the men's breakfast. If she needs firewood, she goes and collects it, if she needs maize she goes to the maize fields to get it or vegetables or whatever she has. She goes and comes back, carrying her child on her back or on her front, then she cooks. That's her day from dawn until dusk, Monday to Sunday. The men in the communities at least have the chance to go and have fun on Sundays, they play basketball or cards. But the women don't stop all day long, there is no rest for them.

What is their entertainment?

'Nothing. There's nothing.'

Ana María continues:

- Since we were kids we started carrying our little brothers around, helping to grind the maize and make *tortillas*, sweep the house or do the washing. There is no chance to go to school, even if there is one in the village, because we have to help mother. And our mothers are obliged to leave the girls at home looking after the baby while they go to work in the maize field. She leaves her baby in the care of the eldest daughter, and the girl drops out of school because she has to look after her little brother, she has to help her mother and that's what happened to me, that's been my life.

Indigenous girls and boys begin their working lives very young. Norma, one of the health service personnel of the EZLN, recounts how when her parents went to the coffee plantation they would carry her on their backs and she also would pick coffee, sitting on her mother's shoulders. 'We began to pick coffee because we were forced to'.

Children are forced to work instead of play, to communicate with adults instead of dolls. Like many others Norma recalls her life in the village:

- I had four smaller brothers and sisters that I had to wash and dress and feed because my mother also went off to work in the fields with my father and brothers. She left me in charge of the kitchen making the *tortillas*. It's really hard, when you are so young, to know what to do, but we learn from our mothers.

There are certainly some tasks which are reserved for the girls: cooking, washing, the children, the housework. However 'men's work' is also done by women and girls when need be. Here again we see the dual burden borne by the female sex. Norma continues her story:

31

- When I was about seven or eight my father said to me 'well, you are old enough now, you have to help me in my work'. So I began to use the machete, to cut the maize, to separate the cob, carry the maize, sow maize and beans. Everything a man does a woman can do just the same, even in the fields. If the maize field is close we leave home at six in the morning. If it is further away, then four o'clock and we stay until six in the evening. And after that we women have to cook the maize, collect water, sew, do everything we weren't able to do during the day. Sometimes we don't even have time to sleep.

The EZLN enters the communities

Five years ago Norma left home for the ranks of the EZLN. Curiously enough it was her mother who had no hesitation in sharing her Zapatista sympathies. Her older son had joined and she managed to convince the father also. Says Norma:

- When I was about twelve the organisation came to my father via my brother, who is the eldest. My father didn't understand the organisation. But it so happened that my mother did understand and she began explaining to us bit by bit. Finally, later, my father came to understand it too and gave us lessons in politics, late at night, telling us how exploited we were. I was still young then.

The EZLN entered the villages in the forest this way, through the family, penetrating it with the community's complicity, ensuring silence and the enrolment of new members. It was a time of secrecy: secrecy that lasted for ten years. Both supporters and non-supporters of the armed struggle were accomplices to this silence. Men, women and children kept silent, paving the way for the surprise attack of January 1st 1994.

Concepción Villafuerte, Director of San Cristóbal de Las Casas' newspaper *El Tiempo,* has her own theory of what happened. She does not have an idealised view of the indigenous people: 'The Indians are bastards, they never accept a *ladino'.* Then she reflects:

-If there's something they don't forgive it is betrayal. You can sell yourself, take advantage of someone, but what you can't do is betray or tell on them, because they will search for you and kill you. The Indians are like that, you can do anything but that. If the EZLN grew for more than ten years, that's why.

The EZLN's paper, *El Despertador Mexicano*, gives an alternative explanation of this slow accumulation of forces. The February 1994 issue editorialised:

It must be clear that, while the civilian organisation can be open, the development of the military side had to be undertaken in silence. This is not easy, but we think we have shown in Chiapas that it is possible, because the creation and development of our army was a secret that thousands and thousands of men, women and children shared and kept over a huge area, where we don't know everybody, and don't even speak the same language as some villagers.

This reveals the amazing interpenetration of the Zapatista people and their army. It was the community-supported Revolutionary Indigenous Clandestine Committees, not just the rebel military command, which were the political leadership in the war of liberation.

During the EZLN gestation period, the existence of a popular guerrilla force in the forest was an open secret. In May 1993 a detachment of the Mexican army bumped into a rebel encampment, Las Calabazas, in the Corralchen mountain range. There they found all sorts of things that gave them an idea of what was brewing: a small-scale reproduction of Ocosingo's main square, uniforms, manuals and much else.

Why did the government of Carlos Salinas do nothing to stop the guerrillas? Perhaps he underestimated their number and did not wish to make it public knowledge that Mexico shared the same problems as other Latin American countries. Mexico was getting ready to sign the Free Trade Agreement with the United States and Canada, with which Salinas figured he would earn a place in the history books 'without getting his hands dirty', as Major Mario of the EZLN would say.

Some of the insurgents point out that during the years prior to the uprising they were already wearing Zapatista uniforms and while they took them off to go down to the villages, often they bumped into people when they were moving from place to place, laden with military equipment. The land-owners and cattle-ranchers wearied of reporting this evidence and being completely ignored by both state and federal governments. However, Salinas didn't get home and dry either. A year before his mandate concluded, the ignored conflict simmering down in the south-east exploded violently. He could no longer close his eyes to it.

The EZLN: a way for women to improve their situation

Rebel Subcomandante Marcos explains that their 'ideology' was communicated thanks to a continuous flow of young girls into the Zapatista Army:

- Those who couldn't cope with life in the mountains went back to their communities and taught and passed on everything they learned. Now entire communities are Zapatistas, even the dogs!

Twenty-nine year-old Rebel Major Ana María, who holds the highest military rank in Los Altos de Chiapas area, describes what the EZLN means to them. In an interview conducted by four female reporters in San Cristóbal de las Casas' cathedral, during the first peace talks in February 1994, she told us:

- Many women go for this because they see they have no rights in their own community, they have no right to education, to do better. They are kept almost blindfolded, unable to learn anything; they are battered and exploited. I mean, the exploitation men suffer, women suffer more, because they are much more marginalised.

The life of marginalisation, of total neglect, is one of continuous sacrifice and sorrow. Moisés, a Tojolabal *campesino* whose village is only accessible in the rainy season by mule, explained to us one rainy night that he is in the struggle 'so that my children can get to try other kinds of food, not just maize, because we eat worse than animals, worse than dogs and we are people'. His wife cries when there's nothing to feed the children, he says. And how else can a mother feel when she is trying to feed her family with every day, cooking day after day the same beans (if there are any), the same *tortillas* on the same old *comal*, the same blackened pot, without any variation because poverty won't allow for it?

Women sacrifice the most: less food on their plate, the worst adult malnutrition levels. Rosario is a young girl from an indigenous village. She is eighteen and pregnant for the second time. Her eldest son is almost two years old now and still breastfeeding. Rosario has to give her breasts to the little one's voracious mouth. She has to work, carry water, fetch firewood and grind the *nixtamal* (maize dough). The baby in her womb is absorbing from her everything she eats. What will be left of this woman's body on which two little children rely and live? How many times will she become pregnant? How many times will she give birth and how many times will she survive it? How many of her children will 'make it', as they say of the children who manage to survive beyond six years of age?

To see a child 'make it' is a tremendous hope for mothers. It is their own small victory against the prevailing conditions in which they suffer. Yet, what about the children who fall sick, die, or become disabled for life? The profound sadness of women who don't manage to save their children can turn into rebellion: 'If I weren't so poor, my son would have made it, but we can't afford medicines nor a doctor nor proper food, nothing', says Filiberta, 'that's why I joined the struggle'.

To make matters worse, machismo is the custom in indigenous communities and it's only just beginning to change in the most advanced rebel ones. Major Ana María pointed out:

- They push us aside. I'm talking about the *compañeras* in the towns and all the women in our country who are suffering the same injustices. But we are capable, we can do other things beside housework and raising children. We can learn.

Learning is also the great attraction of the EZLN for the young women. When they enrol as rebels they all have to learn to speak Spanish, the language of communication in an army of different ethnic groups, the language of established power, to defend themselves against that power.

The EZLN provides opportunities to learn to read and write and to learn history and politics, meet other people, share cultural interests, set up drama groups, write songs, enrol in the different 'youth groups' that later will play at the village parties and who are the young militia and rebel boys and girls in their 'cultural' incarnation.

Within the Zapatista ranks, women demonstrate their intelligence, their ability to command, and a different sense of responsibility, 'and we learn masses of things', says Rigoberta.

- I'm the only woman who has left my village, for study or any other reason that isn't marriage,' says Captain Irma. 'Basically, because of the bourgeois idea that women mustn't know more than men. Here in the EZLN we are all equal. They taught me Spanish, I knew very little when I came, I could understand it but didn't speak it, I didn't know how to read either.

Twenty-three year-old Captain Laura saw the EZLN as the way to improve herself: 'I wanted to be trained, to learn to fight.' Although she was involved in organising women, she wanted to do something more, to learn, to progress. Not just for herself, but for everyone.

- In the mountains we learned many different things, history, for example. The first things the *compañeros* taught were rules, discipline, then to read and write, to speak Spanish well and also military training, cleaning and taking care of your gun...

It's not all study. As journalist Gloria Muñoz pointed out, for many of them the EZLN also means their first sanitary towel. Twenty-three year-old Azucena told Gloria Muñoz of when she lived in her village and didn't even know about sanitary towels.

- It feels awful to have blood dripping down your legs when you are menstruating.

The Zapatista military chief, Subcomandante Marcos, makes the point that there are almost no desertions among women combatants. Perhaps it is because the idea of going back to their own villages, to the house, to the labours accorded to their sex, isn't very attractive for them once they've tasted a different lifestyle. The rebel women have been treated as equals, they can get married, live together, divorce, they can take control of their lives. The idea of returning to the

36

control by the male family members, be it a husband, father or brother, does not appeal.

Levels of participation in the EZLN

In *El Despertador Mexicano* there is a description of the EZLN grassroots supporters.

- In fact, our organised support for the war is the same as our civilian political support. We solve problems for the rebel army: logistics, supplies, information, recruitment, all those tasks.

The role of the women in the Zapatista villages is and has been fundamental throughout. Rebel Major Ana María gives an example of their importance:

- When the EZLN began to grow, the women's role in security became very important. There are bases in each village and we have a communications network. It is the women's job to check security, so that if soldiers arrive they warn us; they operate civil frequency band radios and notify us of any danger or any federal troop movement. This work is undertaken by women, housewives. When we attacked on 1 January 1994, they stayed behind caring for the community, the children and everyone else, while the teenage girls, the daughters, went off to fight.

Women also do many other jobs, they participate directly in the EZLN's tailoring workshops, where they patiently sew the rebel uniforms. There are also female hands in the armoury, where pieces for the guns, munitions and other equipment are manufactured. Any woman from any town in Chiapas, with the insurgency or not, has had the opportunity to spend a while on such tasks.

Drawing on his pipe, Marcos adds:

- It is women who nourish our army, it is they who tell their sons and daughters to join the fight, that it is a good thing and must keep going. It is they who cover up for their relatives when they steal away secretly. It is they who support us, feed us, who toast the *tortillas*, prepare the beans, crush the brown sugar loaf *(piloncillo)* and send it to us in the mountains. When there's a party and they make *tamales*, they always make some extra for the Zapatistas.

37

- If we can survive it is largely because of them. We grow in the communities because of them. In many cases, it was them who pushed the men to vote for war.

The Zapatista chief adds:

- Women are important ideologically in the EZLN and also socially for the EZLN's material and spiritual sustenance. If the women are on our side, the mothers, sisters, daughters, then we are fine.

It is possible to be involved in different ways in the armed struggle and there is a female presence throughout. Whether in the Zapatista Army, with its military hierarchy, guns and barracks life, as a guerrilla fighter in the mountains, or in the Revolutionary Indigenous Clandestine Committees, which bring together people of the highest moral standing in the towns and regions. Comandante Susana is a good example. She was elected as representative for the Tzotzil village women because of her political organising work, not for her ability in handling guns. On the other hand, Maribel holds the rank of captain because of her military responsibility, knowledge and commanding ability. Susana, like Comandante Ramona, lives in her community and visits all the areas where her mother tongue is spoken. Maribel, like Norma or Ana María, lives in the mountains with the rest of the Zapatista troops and devotes all her time 'to the armed revolution'. Generally the rebels are younger, they are from sixteen to no more than thirty years old. The women and men in the Committee are usually over thirty - which among the indigenous people means being a mature adult and in some cases a grandparent – and are the channel between public opinion, communities' thinking and the highest insurgent command.

'They tell us what to do', explains Major Ana María.

- For example, they have to decide if we are going to fight. They consult with the people about what they want done and then come to us and say: 'the people want to do this', and we do it.

Besides the Committee and the insurgents, there are also the Mexican Militia Forces, the people from the towns who have had armed instruction and who are incorporated into the rebel troops when necessary. The militia live their daily lives as *campesinos* and they drill regularly with the rebel command. Every month or two, the militia spend a week in the mountains, at a camp. Then they go back to their village and another group goes. The militias make up the bulk of the Zapatista troops. There are very few women, in contrast to the full-time insurgents. Social acceptance is more difficult: either she lives like a soldier or like a *campesina*, there's no middle ground and the two things aren't easy to combine. Once having worn trousers, boots and shouldered a rifle, to go barefoot again and make *tortillas* like a selfless wife seems far away. Nevertheless, many rebel women did spend some time as militia-women at the beginning, until they decided to stay and become part of the regular army.

The majority of women are involved at the Zapatista base. There, as Marcos would say, is where mothers, old ladies and small girls play a very important role. Their lifestyle does not change, they simply accomplish a series of duties for the organisation and go to assemblies, keep informed and organised.

Ana María, her face covered by her grey balaclava, explains:

- No one is forced to take up a gun or participate in this struggle: it's voluntary. People enter this fight voluntarily and if they don't want to fight they participate in a supporting role. There are many civilians who are not in the movement and that is no problem, we fight for everyone. If land is to be distributed we'll all get some, not only the Zapatistas. Schools, hospitals, and so on, we're all going to benefit, that's what our struggle is about.

The youngest rebel women I met were fifteen or sixteen years old. Ana María says:

- We have a lot of boys and girls in the militia now. There are eight or nine-year-old kids who are restless, they see a rebel and want to touch the gun and play at being Zapatistas. The children come to meetings and sometimes they get upset because we tell them they can't play with the guns until they grow up. Then we have to accept them, of course we don't take them off to fight, but many of them get stubborn and say 'I want to go', that's why there were some in the occupation of San Cristóbal.

According to Subcomandante Marcos, children in the indigenous communities participate in community life and have the right to vote in assemblies from the moment they no longer fall asleep as they are happening!

The young women arrive in the mountains

Major Ana María, a Chol, was one of two female representatives, together with Comandante Ramona, at the first talks at San Cristóbal Cathedral. In perfect Spanish she said:

- I joined the EZLN when I was very young, about fourteen. When I left home and found out there was an armed organisation I made up my mind. One of my brothers was already there, but my parents and most of my family didn't know. I spent many years participating and learning without my family realising. Some *compas* who were a little more educated taught us our alphabet, then we began to learn combat techniques and politics so we could talk to the people and explain our cause to them.

- What made up my mind? It's a very long story.

- I had joined in peaceful protests since I was small. My family are people who had always been organising and struggling to have a decent life, which we never had. We went to the marches and were in an organisation with other villages. We children went too and I started participating when I was eight years old. So from early on my experience was that we will never get anything from peaceful protest. It took years for the people to realise that. The only option left was armed struggle.

Land occupations and community protest were met by government repression. 'We realised that we had to take up arms to defend ourselves', says Ana María.

She was one of the first rebel women when the EZLN was founded:

- At the beginning there were only two of us in the Zapatista army. It was tiny, just eight or ten people, that was in about 1984. Gradually more people joined as people became more politically aware and understood it was necessary to take up arms. They began to join up voluntarily until we were able to form a company, then a battalion, then a regiment. And that's how it kept on growing, until

40

we saw we were strong enough and the people themselves decided to begin to fight.

Women were attracted to the EZLN by the presence of other women:

- They told me and the other *compañera* who joined at the same time as me, that it was because of us that more women have enrolled. Seeing our participation, they saw it was possible and so more *compañeras* entered. Women from the villages began to instruct their daughters, sisters or granddaughters, saying: 'it is better to take a gun and fight'.

It is not an easy decision for a young indigenous girl. Joining the guerrilla is like a leap in the dark. For Irma, going to live in the mountains was a big change.

- First you are sad to leave your family, but then you begin to learn and cheer up knowing something will come out of your effort, struggling for a cause that someday we will win, for women, for everyone.

Young girls start a radically different life in the EZLN, which is very tough at the beginning:

- It gets easier with time, you have to forget the things you left behind. The *compañeros* teach you, we talk together; it's like a family again, we learn to love each other because our brothers and sisters stayed on the other side and that brings us together.

Laura recounts her first years with the rebels and how she looked for support to her *compañeras*.

- At the beginning it is hard to get used to it, your family isn't there, everything is different. When I joined there were several women, and of course, somehow you get in touch. They help you out, you feel sad and low, but you get used to living with men, to seeing the world differently. Besides, things were already changing in my village, people's awareness of women's situation and of the need for equality for all was growing.

The insurgents can't go back to visit their parents whenever they want to, often they are stationed far from their birthplace. Laura, for example, hadn't seen her family for three and a half years:

- Do I feel like seeing them? I don't mind, well it would be nice, but look, we are at war. My *compañeros* are like my family now. With the *compas* you relax, you share lots of things, they help you... It's as if they were your brothers, your superior officers are like your parents, the ones who have been here longest are your elder brothers...

Captain Elisa, a young Tzeltal girl, agrees:

- When I came here I got used to it bit by bit, of course sometimes you miss your family, but the compas cheered me up and I was no longer homesick. Before the first of January I used to visit my family every year. I didn't tell them this was going to happen, they knew anyway, but they didn't try and keep me at home, quite the contrary, they encouraged me to keep going and supported me. One of my brothers is in the EZLN too. We enrolled together but they separated us and I haven't heard from him since.

Laura has never considered leaving the EZLN, even though she confesses that life in the mountains is very hard. Asked what is most difficult, she answers resoundingly:

- *Everything*: cooking, laying a fire, the exercises... and the marches. When I start to walk I get this sore throat and it hurts, that's the worst for me. Sometimes we walk seven or eight hours with our backpacks, climbing up and down.

Ana María adds:

- Women do the same things as men, learning combat techniques, doing political work in the villages...

- There is respect in our organisation, especially among the combatants. In the communities the old ideas prevail, violence and beatings, but there is a lot of equality in our ranks. The work men do women can do, the education we get is the same, also the degree of responsibility we can achieve. I, for example, hold the rank of insurgent Major of Infantry. I command a battalion, I lead them in battle and I know I can lead my people. I proved that in the occupation of San Cristóbal.

Ana María is obeyed by thousands of Zapatistas of both sexes. Nevertheless, one might suppose that it must be difficult for men to take orders from a woman...

- Sometimes we joke and tell the *compañeros* to behave 'like real men'. Machismo still crops up but we are trying to stop it. The new *compañeros* find it really hard to take orders from a woman, it seems all wrong and they aren't used to it. But they do get used to it. The *compañeros* who have been here longer think it's normal, they see how important women's participation is in our struggle.

Chapter 3

Of love, marriage, children and war

EZLN women have challenged indigenous tradition deeply on gender issues. They can decide not to take a husband and as soldiers they must avoid getting pregnant, although they do not renounce sexual activity. It is a million miles from village life, where a girl is expected to get married and have children.

Major Ana María is very familiar with this reality:

- They get married very young, at thirteen or fourteen, often against their will. That's why the EZLN Revolutionary Law on Women includes the right to choose a partner without obligation. This law was proposed by the women from the villages and we all supported it. In some places, if a young man likes a young girl he doesn't go and ask her if she likes him, but goes straight to her father and asks to have her. He brings along a litre of rum and says: 'I want your daughter'. By the time the girl realises, she's already been sold off. The women are forced violently. Many women cry their way to the groom's house or to the altar, you know, because they don't want to, they don't agree. You can't just have a boyfriend or date like in the city, tradition makes that a sin.

The wedding tradition of the Tzotziles in Los Altos de Chiapas is a lengthy procedure. In the testimonial book *A Wedding in Zinacantan*, by Juan de la Torre López, Anselmo Pérez explains:

- Many years ago, when a young boy reached engagement age, first he offered his respects to his father and mother, presenting them with a bottle of rum, and requesting they ask for the hand of the girl on his behalf.

If they agree to do so, the boy's parents gather six or seven 'Jak'oletik' or 'askers' and their wives, plus an old lady to take charge of delivering the presents to the bride's father, another lady to take charge of the drinks and three more men to pour the rum. The ritual of visiting the girl's home takes a long time while her father is treated with food, fruits, favours and most of all, rum. The only one who doesn't appear at all in the traditional wedding is the bride, who is totally overlooked. Says Anselmo Pérez:

- They don't ask their daughter whether she wants to marry or not: the father and mother decide.

A positive answer leads to courtship. However, the bride doesn't get close to the groom at any time, they don't even exchange a word. It's her father who the groom has to please, to whom he gives presents, whom he chats with, in whose company he drinks a lot of rum and for whom he will labour for several months. This was the old traditional way. In some ways it did provide some knowledge of the man to whom the daughter was to be given and she at least got used to seeing him during 'courtship'.

But the passing of time, and poverty, allowed only the worst of the old traditions to persist. The father considers himself the lord and master of his daughters and selling them at any point is socially acceptable, as can be seen in Hacia el Ahlan K'inal (already mentioned). Dominga, from Huixtán, didn't want to go with her parents to settle the forest. Her mother says:

- My husband got pissed off because Dominga didn't obey. So he talked to a man who was asking to marry her. If she doesn't come along I'm going to sell her to that man, he thought. Dominga didn't want to get married, but since my husband had the money already she went away in tears with her new husband.

After the uprising, assemblies were held to discuss women's rights. They complained of their parents' harshness in arranging their daughters' marriage:

- Sometimes girls are asked for when they are still very young, and the parents don't think clearly, they sell the daughter for money, or give her away to a man when she is just eleven or twelve years old. A girl that age can't cope with the duty of looking after a husband and she goes back home. Parents who understand this wouldn't marry us off before we are grown-ups because it is very difficult to look after a husband and children when we are poor.

But what chance of avoiding her destiny does a girl have when

45

she's already been sold by her father to a man she doesn't like? With the rigid social rules of the indigenous communities, none. Where to run to? How to face the terror of a first night with a man she does not know or love?

Captain Irma found a way of dealing with the impasse. She ran off along with her brother and joined the ranks of the EZLN. There, some years later, she fell in love with and married a rebel.

In May 1994 indigenous women gathered together in San Cristóbal and pronounced themselves in agreement with the Zapatista law that says they can't be forced to marry.

- Before, women were exchanged for a cow. But marriage has to be the woman's free choice.

Some concluded:

- When we don't want to marry, it is better to discuss it with our parents and the man and not be forced, because that ruins a girl's life, especially when children come later on.

The picture is not always so bleak. Juana Hernandez, from San Juan Chamula municipality, recounts how lucky she was:

- I married of my own free will, my mother didn't force me. Our custom is just to live together, no church or registry office.

A seventeen-year-old Tzotzil boy, Pedro, who works as a gardener, asked me one morning for some money. He needed fifty pesos to buy all the things his father-in-law requested in exchange for his daughter: four cases of soft drinks, eight kilos of meat, five kilos of sugar, ten litres of rum, three bags of coffee. She is also seventeen and according to Pedro, in order to get her to marry him he abducted her: 'I took her out of her house, just like that', but he points out it was with her agreement.

- The thing is, I don't have a father, my father drank a lot of rum and he died. I started working when I was just eight, that's how I learned to work. My mother and my brothers and I all became Protestants.

Now Pedro has to pay the dowry to his partner's father and that will formalise the marriage, they won't go to a church or a registry office. At the beginning the father-in-law was requesting money, but with the help of María Auxiliadora, a Protestant pastor in the

46

neighbourhood of San Cristóbal, he was convinced to follow custom and take goods instead. Pedro says that if he has a daughter he will do the same, he'll demand a dowry.

The anthropologist Andrés Medina discusses the common practice of abduction (which is also rape in many cases) as a way of getting married, in *Tenejapa: Family and Traditions of a Tzeltal Town*.

- Abduction is another way of reducing the burden of the dowry. It usually takes place at village parties. The prospective boyfriend keeps an eye on the girl he likes and goes to wait for her on her way back home and at the right moment he grabs her and takes her off into a field, where they will spend the night. This happens after the girl has accepted the male's courtship. The day after the abduction, the boyfriend will go to her house to talk to her relatives, bringing several litres of rum and hoping for a positive reception, because her relatives can take revenge and beat him up. Some *ladinos* from the town say that years ago abduction of women was more frequent and spectacular, the women being grabbed in the market and dragged off to the man's house.

Hell at the in-laws

When an indigenous woman gets married she has no preparation for sex, because reproductive issues and anything erotic are taboo. They face this experience alone, when they are still little more than children.

Furthermore, men have been educated in such a way that they would never feel required to show any special care or give any kind of explanation to their wives. They simply 'use them' as one often hears it said. One night, hardly containing her laughter, Azucena asked us, men and women alike: 'What about you, have you been used?' Although as a Zapatista she lives another way of life and while she was directing her question to a male photographer, the expression is indicative in that it usually refers to women.

Sexual pleasure is unknown to them, 'that is not done, it's not traditional', asserted Sebastiana fiercely during the late 1995 government negotiations. To make matters worse for the newly-wed, tradition dictates that she live with her in-laws. Overnight the young girls become the focus of the suspicion of an alien household and are often exploited too. Far from their mothers and relatives, they enter a universe in which they are strangers. Often, however hard they try, they will be treated with contempt. Women say that it is common for 'the in-laws to encourage the husband to beat his wife'. In most cases, they agree, 'my husband's family and my husband take me for a servant'.

Women are brought up to put up with everything uncomplainingly. The speech of the bride's parents in the Tzeltal town Oxchuc, on the eve of her departure, goes like this, according to Martín Gómez Ramirez in *Ofrenda a los ancestros en Oxchuc*:

> Now the birthplace will be left forever, for she is leaving for another home, to another house, in other lands, in other places; because her parents so desired, they have allowed it to be so, now her husband's parents will become hers. Now listen, my girl, to what I'm about to tell you, hear what my lips say, what my heart commands: 'So, my daughter, be good, put your best foot forward, don't gossip, don't lie, don't criticise your father-in-law, don't reproach your mother-in-law either or slander your fellows, or gossip as you go about your business, or swear. Now that you're getting married, obey the commands of your father-in-law, your mother-in-law, your husband, don't ever be arrogant. Listen first to what you are told, so that you can comply correctly. Only in that way will they be content, only if you obey with your hands and feet, but if you slander or defame your father-in-law, judge your mother in-law, reproach your fellows, judge your brother-in-law's wife, disrespect your husband, then illness will come, evil will come to your family. Don't call the Devil upon you, don't attract the Devil, please, my daughter. If you have listened to what we've told you I shall be contented, I'll be satisfied because then there won't be gossip nor will you bring shame on our family.

Sometimes however the woman can't bear the situation or is childless. Anthropologist Andrés Medina looks at the causes of separation between Tzeltals, including sterility and the in-laws. In the former case the woman has lost her worth, so she can be returned like defective goods:

> The dissolution of the domestic group by the separation of the couple is a relatively frequent phenomenon in family life. The most critical moment is that between the wedding and the birth of the first child... The absence of children leads to separation, and sterility, in most cases, is blamed on the woman. Separation between a husband and wife with no descendants means that her relatives have to give back all the wedding presents. If there are children, the woman goes back to her parents' home bringing the youngest baby, who needs the mother's milk. If there are older ones, they stay with their father and his family. There are basically two reasons for separation when there are children: failure of either spouse to fulfill familial responsibilities, or conflict between the wife and the husband's relatives, which ends with the woman returning to the parental home.

Deep in the Lacandon forest, in the Tojolabal community of La Realidad, eighteen-year-old Berta has had to go back to her mother's house. While she breast-feeds her daughter and serves beans to her three-year-old son, she wipes away her tears and tells how she ran away from home because she could no longer stand being ill-treated by her in-laws who were given to shouting, constant scolding, malicious gossip and even beating. For young, efficient, intelligent Berta, accustomed to hard work, life became a nightmare. She cried every day, and however hard she tried she couldn't stop her in-laws' criticism. Sometimes Ruth, her mother, came along with her to the maize field. Her beautiful daughter's tears and the purple rings around her eyes made her sad, but she couldn't do anything; that is the custom. One night, Berta decided to go to her mother's with her two children. Her mother, aunt and grandmother live together, three

49

single women who understood the young girl's desperation.

Ruth, Felisa, Teresa and Berta depend upon Ruth's eldest son, who lives with them, plus his wife and a little boy. They carry firewood, help to harvest other people's maize for a small portion of it, load it on their shoulders, look for firewood, sow, plough the land, find a way to get some beans and feed the four small children and a fifth on the way.

Berta was terrified, thinking her husband might come to take away her children. Tradition dictates that the man takes the females and the woman the males, but the girl-baby is still breast-feeding and Berta wanted to keep both of them. It appears that these women from La Realidad have had poor luck in finding a partner. Ruth tells us that her husband was a murderer, a madman who would kill anyone because according to him, a sorcerer had put the evil eye on him. 'They adored Satan because they had no God.' Besides, Ruth wasn't his first wife, he had another wife and he had killed his father-in-law. His violent behaviour is described by Ruth: 'He threatened to kill me too'. The murderer was shot dead. It happened in a community right next to La Realidad, called Guadalupe Los Altos. He was going to finish off a young lad who he decided was bringing misfortune. The lad climbed up a tree to try to escape. His wife was nearby and saw him being shot at and thought he was dead. She ran to tell her family and a group of men went to lay an ambush for Ruth's husband - 'he was hunted like a deer on the road', says Ruth - and his days were over.

Ruth was able to breathe freely from then on. 'He had killed five or six times and drank a lot,' she recalls. She didn't think of getting married again, she was better off alone and of course, had peace of mind, 'and we'll always have a little *pozol* if nothing else' she told herself. 'There were other men who were interested but not enough, because of my family and my children.'

Felisa, Ruth's sister, has a three year-old boy. Her son's father left her for another woman and went to live in Las Margaritas. He's never given her any money to help her support the child. There seems to be little chance of beautiful, thirty year-old Felisa marrying again. The strict social code of a small village refuses an 'abandoned' woman the chance of beginning again. Felisa has thought of looking for a job as a maid in the city, but Teresa, her wise old mother, appeals to her common sense. What will she and her little boy find? Exploitation, pain, hard work, abandonment and only distance from everything they have here, community, family, nature. At least they have *pozol* ... Where in Tuxtla are they going to find *pozol* like they make in La Realidad? And Maseca brand *tortillas*? No way.

Love in the EZLN

It is May 1994. Rigoberta and Captain Cristóbal are together now, assigned to the same unit. Rigoberta is very young, she might be seventeen, Cristóbal, twenty-six. They cuddle and caress furtively from dusk 'till dawn. Other times, she sits on his lap, her arms around his neck. They ask us reporters to take a picture of them before we leave their camp for the city. They want to have a picture of themselves together. They put on their balaclavas, step away from each other and say 'Ready'. It seems they want to be separate but together in the same picture. 'Move closer!' we shout; and shyly one of them puts the arm around the other's shoulder. It doesn't matter. A picture of them rolling around together in a corner of the camp would have been better. Never mind, in the picture their eyes, the only exposed bit of their faces, are shining with all the love, happiness and hope in the world.

Quick-witted, wisecracking Captain Maribel explains how lovers get engaged in the Zapatista army:

- When a *compañero* loves a *compañera*, the first thing he has to do is ask the commanding officer for permission. 'Well, I like that *compañera*, I love her.' Then when he goes to talk to her, she already knows he has permission. Why ask the commanding officer? Well because that way they find out if another *compañero* is already involved.

Maribel has been a rebel for nine years. There are more ways, she explains:

- There are two ways here in the EZLN: one is that the couple gets together and that's it, we have a party and celebrate, we already know they are married and therefore the couple has to be respected. The other way is that they sign an agreement saying they're getting married of their own free will, that nobody forced them to and that the most important thing in their relationship will be their work and not their partner. We women in the EZLN know that our work is what has to be done well, because we won't be here forever together. Sometimes the *compañero* has to go to work in one place and the *compañera* in another. Or it can happen that the *compañero* is a captain and so is the *compañera* and they have to stick to their units. Then they just meet when there's a chance to be together. That also causes trouble, because sometimes the man gets uptight imagining what his *compañera* might be doing... They imagine all sorts of things. But we correct mistakes collectively, so that problems can be dealt with out in the open.

Maribel tells of the significance of collective participation in the ritual:

- When the *compañeros* sign the agreement, the commanding officers present stand to attention with those of us at the celebration, we cross our rifles and they walk underneath. This also means that we defend their marriage and we are happy fighting along with them and we have a party and - bingo! - they are married.

The rebel troops in Los Altos have the same practice. The commanding officer of the area narrates:

- If someone wants to get married, if a woman likes a *compañero*, she goes and asks permission of the commanding officer to see if she can get him to go out with her and if a man likes a *compañera* he asks permission and the officer says yes or no, and first they have to check if the *compañera* or the *compañero* is already taken.

Traditional indigenous communities are shocked at the ease with which people get together in the EZLN. Explains Ana María:

- In the EZ, if we are attracted to a *compañero*, we are given permission to get to know each other for a while, to go out together and then perhaps decide to get married.

Permission may be given for a couple to be married in a religious ceremony, with their family present, but it depends on the particular circumstances. Divorce is not penalised, the couple just split up and communicate the fact to their superior officer. Also, if a woman says

52

'I do not want to be with so-and-so anymore' and he goes on harassing her, the officer will separate them in order to avoid trouble.

Mixed marriages between rebels and civilians are also occurring. In January 1995, a year after the uprising and a month before the February military raid, Captain Maribel said:

- Not long ago a *compañero* got married, here in town. First of all we had to ask for the parents' permission. Then the guy and the girl started dating and we began to prepare a party with the whole community and then they got married. However, the *compañera* has to join the rebel ranks. In this case, she had already thought of becoming a member of the EZLN so it wasn't a problem, she was ready to do that, she was part of the militia.

During the thirteen months when the EZLN 'liberated' a large part of the forest, the rebels co-existed with the villagers. According to Maribel, who is head of the youth group in charge of cultural activities, dances, theatre and Zapatista songs, the young girls from various communities joined the militia.

- All the young girls came into the militia, of course there were those who don't want to and don't, it all depends on the person. They said: 'I'm going to participate here, and go step by step', that's how the *compañeras* participate. So we start to see co-existence between rebels and civilians. It's a good thing, because the community itself understands and supports it.

Have you married? Captain Maribel answers:

- Yes. I decided to have a relationship with a *compañero*, I got married, with permission and in front of all the *compañeros*. However, there are always difficulties, we had problems, wanted to get divorced and we did, no problem.

That is as much as she wishes to say about her personal life. In another forest ravine, in 1994, Lieutenant Azucena says:

- I got married three years ago, on May the 13th. The *compañeros* lined up, crossed their rifles and Captain Martin and I walked underneath. We signed an agreement and they threw a party with food. But even if you get married it isn't like in the villages - we are soldiers, and you know sometimes we'll get together but each one has his job and it mustn't matter if your husband goes away.

Maternity, contraception and abortion

In Chiapas maternity is seen as a woman's primary mission. When a young woman gets married she knows she has to 'give children'. If for any physical reason she is incapable of having children, she becomes a frustrated woman and is viewed as such by all. Marriage, often loveless, is in reality a socio-economic contract based upon procreation. It is believed that fertility is a divine blessing, granted by that ultimate female deity, the moon. Women who can't have children are punished by the gods, they are excluded and are frequently the object of contempt.

One of the characters in *Oficio de tinieblas*, by Rosario Castellanos, tackles the social issue of infertile women:

> Catalina Diaz Puiljá, at twenty years already withered and aged, had been gifted to Pedro by her parents from childhood. At first there was happiness. Being without a child was seen as natural. However, later, when the girls she spun with, carried water and firewood with, started walking with heavier tread (carrying their own weight and that of the one inside them), when their eyes softened and their bellies swelled up like balloons, then Catalina touched her empty hips, hated her light step and looking quickly behind her saw that she had left no footprint. She became distressed, thinking that she would be remembered thus by the village. From then onwards she could not find rest [...] And the moon didn't turn white, as for the women who conceive, but was tinted red like the moon of the spinsters and widows and the women of pleasure.

The Mayans say that women's fertility depends on the moon. Its cycles presage the human and agricultural reproductive cycle. The moon is the holy mother, 'ch'ul metik' - in Tzotzil - the mother of the sun. A full moon is considered the best moment for conception and therefore for sexual relations. 'Some indigenous people believe most women menstruate during the new moon and are more fertile at full moon', explains William Holland in *Mayan Medicine in Los Altos de Chiapas*.

54

Sex for procreation within marriage is what is considered normal. Everything else is considered a sin by most people.

Lawyer Marta Figueroa stresses the importance of reproduction:

- If you sterilise indigenous women you take away the only value they have in the eyes of the community, therefore they can no longer be part of the community.

The Zapatistas, however, came to shake up the old order of things. The rebels are girls of reproductive age who renounce this stage of womanhood to devote themselves to the struggle, without renouncing sex. An abyss separates them from the parochial mindset of their mothers. 'We can't have children in the Zapatista Army. We use condoms', says twenty-year-old Azucena, amused.

Captain Maribel adds:

- We can't have children here because conditions do not permit it. We can't look after them. However, some *compañeras* have got pregnant, they go back to their communities to have the child, then they decide whether they want to come back.

She stresses that the girls choose their contraceptive method.

- The pill or injections, whichever she wants. At the beginning we had trouble getting them, but recently - January 1995 - some *compañeras* have given us some more.

The pill can have side effects. Many of the women are rounded, maybe because in the EZLN they have regular daily food, which they didn't have in their villages or maybe it is due to the monotonous diet. Maribel agrees:

- Yes, it is hard with the pill, because at the beginning we all get headaches, but after a while the *compañeras* get used to them.

Major Ana María explains that the army women are an exception:

- In the rebel army we can't have children because we are constantly on duty, moving from one place to another and because our job is to fight for the people. It would be very difficult to bring up a baby in the mountains. Therefore, we have family planning. However, if a *compañera* wants to have a baby, she goes to live with her family and has it. If she wants to come back afterwards she leaves her mother or her mother in-law to look after the baby. There have been many cases in which *compañeras* have got pregnant by accident, they've had the baby and left it with their family because they want to continue in the struggle.

Contraceptives are available in the EZLN, but according to Ana María, in the indigenous communities, 'they don't exist, they are unknown'.

On the issue of abortion she adds:

- Parents are careful that their daughters do not get pregnant. Young girls are so afraid of their parents that they don't even talk to boys. Nevertheless, many girls do get pregnant and they have the baby, but it isn't easy to get an abortion and if someone does have one she doesn't tell... Abortion is an issue we don't discuss or mention at all. There is a belief that abortion is wrong. It would be like perverting tradition.

A reporter from *La Jornada* asked Ana María, in the cathedral in San Cristóbal, what happens if they have the possibility to abort, as one out of five women of fertile age in rural Mexico has had an abortion. She answered:

- The fact that a tradition or a belief exists doesn't mean it can't change. For now it is not allowed in the communities, it's punished, women who abort are punished. What happens often is that the girl goes to a midwife or a natural healer and asks to have an abortion for fear of her family and of being beaten. In the communities that I know of, the people doing it are fined or they catch the man who got her pregnant and lock him up for a few days and then fine him or make him pay for the girl's medical care.

Traditional medicine

In Los Altos de Chiapas, in contrast to elsewhere in Mexico, female mortality is higher than male mortality. Many die in childbirth. There are no reliable statistics, however, because many indigenous women do not have a birth certificate. And in such cases, no one bothers to register the death, because 'they didn't exist'. In her *Indigenous Medical Practice,* Graciela Freyermuth writes that in Chamula death during pregnancy is covered up and other causes given officially. It is also a curious fact that women never tell their husbands about pregnancy because they consider it shameful.

The indigenous concept of health embraces more than the physical condition, including relations with one's neighbours, religious responsibilities and upholding tradition.

> If you steal or kill then you have sexual dreams. If you speak badly of someone or neglect your duties or argue with your neighbours then illness follows.

In Los Altos people also think that you can catch a disease on the road because of jealousy, you can fall down and 'lose your spirit into the earth', because of dreams or witchcraft. The power of physical and spiritual healing is attributed to the *ilol*, an experienced natural healer. Knowledge is usually passed from one generation to the next. As Freyermuth writes, an *ilol* 'knows which [diseases] have been caused by the wind, the thunder, the devil or water or through dreams, envy, food or non-acceptable social behaviour. Through the pulse he can feel a blood current going to the heart and mind.' The *ilols* claim they can find out everything related to the patient, from the illness itself to the social rule transgressed. They use magic, herbs, fortune telling, laying-on of hands and some allopathic medicines.

> The *ilol* uses a wide range of treatments. There are rites such as calling the lost soul, passing the handle of the corn-grinding stone over the pregnant woman's body during prolonged labour or sacrificing hens; prayers in caves, at church, at home, or where the disease was caught; or else candles, rum, 'blowing', physical manipulation, animals, stones and most of all plants can be used. The latter can be either drunk as tea, or eaten raw, ground with water or made into a paste, used in baths, suppositories, powders, or heated on the comal.

The healer also decides in which direction the altar has to be set so that the prayer will bring about the cure, what colour and size the candles should be and the right time of day.

When a midwife is also an *ilol* and a herbalist, she is as qualified as you can be in Tzotzil medicine. Her services will be frequently requested and many sick people will call at her house to be treated. She charges very little. Working as an *ilol* allows a woman to expand her knowledge and the areas she can work in.

A very important element of the indigenous cosmology is the belief in a lower world, a hell, and a series of threatening forces which loom over the lives of men and women. There is a sense of fatality that at the same time acts as an iron form of social control. Any infraction of community rules will be punished by supernatural forces. Researcher William Holland R. points out in his book *La medicina maya en los altos de Chiapas* that 'someone who cuts himself, falls over, fights a friend, strikes his wife, breaks a bone, loses or forgets something...' is considered a victim of the gods of death.

Mayans believe that when a person is born an animal is also born, which will become his *nagual* or partner throughout his life until death, when they both die. Their destinies are inseparable. The animal and the human share the same spirit if not the same flesh. Whatever happens to one will happen to the other: power, illness, pain or death. The Tzotziles believe that these animals live in sacred mountains, separated into families. When a woman marries a man, her *nagual* leaves its parents' sacred mountain and goes to live at the husband's. If an indigenous man or woman goes to live far away, in the city, and becomes half *ladino,* rejecting indigenous traditions, then their animal partner goes to one of the faraway unknown mountains of the white people. This person will no longer be acknowledged by the Indians as their *nagual* lives elsewhere.

The role of the indigenous midwife

In Chiapas seventy percent of pregnant women in the urban areas go to a midwife, whereas in the countryside the midwife takes care of practically every birth.

- It is believed that the moon decides when the children will be born, so when there's a new moon people say 'the moon has gone to bring more children to the mothers' wombs'. The protection of the moon is requested and is used to determine gestation dates. When a woman feels she is pregnant she looks at the size of the moon, and then calculates nine months. During that time pregnant women pray to the moon for a healthy birth. Prayers are intensified if labour is late (A. Medina, op. cit.).

The Tzotzil have guarded their traditions more zealously than any other group. Childbirth is pretty much forbidden territory for *ladinos* or outsiders. Birth is a ritual ceremony, always accompanied by *posh* - home-made rum - coloured candles, incense and smoke. Women give birth at home, fully clothed. The new-born emerges from between the folds of the *nagua*, the woollen skirt. Tzotzil women rarely give birth laying down, usually they stand or squat, hanging onto their husband's neck - that is his contribution to the labour. Sometimes the father and other relatives take shifts in providing the strenuous support required. The whole family, their guests and the midwife celebrate the birth with prayers, chanting and huge quantities of posh. In the Tzeltal town Tenejapa, Medina writes that, 'birth is a personal occasion witnessed only by the midwife and the husband and sometimes also his mother. The husband supports the woman from behind so she can give birth squatting'.

Indigenous birth rites vary slightly. In Tenejapa:

- The natural healer cuts the umbilical cord off the baby and hangs it from a nearby tree and the placenta is placed on the household fire. The baby is bathed in warm water and the father chews a little chilli, putting a bit of it on the baby's lips to prevent them staying black. For the first three days after the birth the mother rests and the relatives keep company outside, around a makeshift fire. They say this is to prevent the child from 'diseases', because this is when s/he is most exposed... For twenty days the woman drinks warm water and is considered weak.

In the Lacandon forest, traditions are more diluted. In the course of settlement many ancient indigenous traditions were abandoned. Women were forced to face a hostile world, far from any facilities, in an unknown habitat and climate. The first arrivals had to give birth without their mothers, in extreme conditions, in an unfamiliar world.

Teresa, Tojolabal midwife

Teresa arrived with the first settler families. After climbing hills, crossing fields and clearing their path through the undergrowth with machetes, they happened upon the valley they would call La Realidad. It was covered in thick vegetation, huge trees and thick shrubs and there was water. The Tojolabal people had walked for days, carrying their few belongings on their backs: a machete, a blanket, some *tortillas*, and the hope of land. They built La Realidad with their own hands, by the sweat of their brow. Step by step, in that inhospitable valley inhabited by pumas and malaria-carrying insects, humble straw and timber houses were built. With much effort they managed to channel the river that now winds through the village bringing water close to the dwellings. They had created a clearing for settlement.

As time went by Teresa became a grandmother and the town's midwife.

- Nobody taught me, it was something I wanted and was able to do but I only discovered this when I was about thirty years old.

One of this Tojolabal woman's gifts, which the doctors who have met her have been unable to explain, is that she can manipulate babies from breach position in their mother's belly. She has never had to do a caesarean. In addition, Teresa states she has never lost a single child during labour. Who taught her? How did she learn? Teresa dreamed she was making clay pots, she says they were very pretty pots, and she was modelling them with her hands. Later, when she touched the pregnant woman's belly she let herself be led by those dreams and modelled again. Gesturing with her gentle but worn hands she explains:

- Let's say this banana is the baby and it is in breach position - this is the head and this is the bottom. If he is like this inside the mother, you take a little ointment and turn the baby like this to move him down. Then you have to search for the head and turn it round and then lift the bottom into the right position, bottom up and the head in the vagina.

This grey-haired old lady discovered her gift through dreams:

- I don't know what happened, I just dreamed a lot, I dreamed of very pretty little pots, I see them shining and inside them there are like a lot of little ribbons and beads of different colours. It seems it is my fate to become a midwife. Those are my dreams. I believe God gave me a task, a job to do. But I've stopped dreaming since I've become a midwife.

A long history of poverty, isolation and complete absence of medical care led her to discover her ability. Near La Realidad, at Guadalupe Los Altos, where she went often with a niece who was pregnant and who the midwives wanted to have an abortion.

- They have a midwife there, but I don't think she knew what to do. My niece was about four months pregnant. She'd already bought the remedy, a bottle of wine, I don't know what kind and they were going to give it to her to make her abort.

It was superstition that led her to want to get rid of her child:

- Her midwife said the child was an animal, that it wouldn't be human, but a frog or a pig, that was what the people taking care of her said.

So the frightened girl went to see a natural healer and she told her sister-in-law that she would go and get the remedy. 'All right, but be careful', answered the latter. It happened that Teresa had arrived in town that day.

The girl's sister in-law asked her, 'Your aunt arrived yesterday, didn't she? Why don't you talk to her?.'

'Oh, because I don't know if she knows what to do'.

'She does, she took care of me, my baby was in breach position and she turned him around.'

Then the girl, whose name is Margarita, went to ask permission from her father-in-law, 'My aunt Teresa arrived yesterday and she knows how to help. Why don't we ask for her help?'

'Well, dear,' said her father-in-law 'well, if you want to ask for her help I'll do it tomorrow.'

Teresa continues the story:

- The old man didn't delay, he came the next day. At that time my husband didn't know I was delivering babies. As I came back from gathering maize, the old man arrived.

'Where is my little brother?'

'You sit down, he'll be right back.'

'Well, we'll talk when he comes.'

He sat down there with his bag. I wondered: 'why does he want to see my husband?' When my husband arrived with his horse (he had been to get maize), they unloaded and sat down to rest. He took out a big bottle of rum and a glass.

'So, my brother, I come on behalf of your niece, for she says Teresa here knows how to help those who are...pregnant.'

'I know nothing of that'.

My husband turned around and asked me: 'Is it true you know about pregnancy?'

'I don't really know, but I'm learning.'

'If you know how to do it, then help my niece too.'

On the next day I went there. First they gave me coffee. Then I went to see Margarita.

'How are you?'

'I'm pregnant but people say it's not going to be human.'

'How come it won't be human? Isn't the father human then?'

'Yes, but I've been told that maybe it's going to be some sort of frog or a pig.'

'But how can you believe them?'

'Yes, but who knows?'

'Let's see what we can do for you'.

She went to her bed and I looked at her. I told her:

'Don't be afraid, you're all right, you're pregnant, you're all right.'

'Then if I'm all right, I don't have to have an abortion?'

'No, you don't, you're all right and I'm going to help you.'

So I kept visiting her. When she was due I wasn't there, there was another midwife there, a man, and he attended her and she had a healthy baby girl.

Many years have passed since then. Now says Teresa, 'I'm granny to all the children, I have about two hundred grandchildren!'

After that incident her services began to be requested:

- That's how people in my town knew I was a midwife, after the people already knew here. Then they came to ask me for help and to look after their women... I thought to myself: 'how am I going to manage to help the women? And how do I hold the baby?' But then I thought, 'well, I've already been through that, I myself have children, I know my body and other women's bodies are no different.'

She recalls her own childbirths:

- I'm pregnant, I go to get my maize, carry firewood and then I'm in bed, my baby boy or girl is already there with me. When my family notices I've had my baby with me for two days already. It's easy, yes, it is easy to have children. The hard thing is to lose them. I have seven children, but not all of them survived, four died, only three girls survived.

Although Teresa insists she is a midwife by vocation, there is a family tradition, which is often the way:

- My mother and father were midwives and they were good at it as I am now. There are three of us now, my brother and also my sister who is here in Santa Rita now.

A doctor visiting La Realidad was so amazed by her work that he decided to learn from her. He told her:

- 'Well, Doña Teresa, you know your people's ways which is something that no medical course teaches us. You are self-taught but it is also your destiny. You work with me and I'll help you as much as I can.' So I worked with him. He gave me all my equipment, but when he went and other doctors came, I didn't want to continue with them. They weren't good with patients.

Teresa continued to receive pupils; doctors who had graduated from the best Mexican universities. She taught them to deliver babies.

- They came here often, asking for support, and saw how I manipulate babies in breach position and then started to do it too.

In these places, childbirth always takes place at home, in bed, without undressing. Felisa, Teresa's daughter, was horrified that when she was in the hospital she saw women about to give birth wearing just a white gown, open at the back. For an indigenous woman to be undressed by someone else is one of the worst things that can happen to her. Felisa explains:

- We don't take off our clothes here. We give birth the way we are, with clothes on and then you get changed afterwards. The next day they come to bathe us with warm water, at home. In the hospital it's awful...

Teresa carries out a ritual, less complicated than the Tzotzil one:

- When the baby is born a little 'promise' is lighted, a little candle for good health. I bathe him with good soap and warm water and clean him up neatly. I cut the umbilical cord with a razor blade. I dab on surgical spirit, press the cord and tie it up again. The piece attached to the baby has to be tight so it won't bleed. I cut it in the middle, then I cauterise it with a candle so it won't bleed. You wash him well, clean him with a cloth, put the nappy on, the baby vest, shawl, everything. You give him to his mother, who is there lying down. Then he is passed on to the father, the grandfather, each of them give him a kiss and after that, depending on the time, you tell him good morning or good afternoon.

The husband is inside, and witnesses the birth, 'he helps the mother', says Teresa. The floor of the forest huts are made of earth. The placenta will stay there:

- When the baby is ready, we make a hole in the earth and bury the placenta, so it stays inside the house.

-If the baby is born with the umbilical cord tied around his neck, it is because the mother forgot to untie the leather headband she uses when hauling firewood. That's why a pregnant woman has to be mindful of many details. Teresa knows how to use herbs. There aren't any contraceptive herbs, it's against nature. Rather, the herbs are used for the opposite, to beget children, which is the greatest gift. Teresa doesn't have a set fee for deliveries.

- I'm happy because people see that I do my job because I want to. So if they want to they give me ten or five thousand (old) pesos.

Other midwives, men (because there are a few) or women, have set fees. Teresa says that there are people who charge a hundred new pesos for a boy's birth. (One new peso is worth a thousand old pesos). If it happens to be a girl, the price is half, fifty new pesos. The *campesinos* always prefer to have a boy than a girl.

The names for the new-borns are chosen by the family; their favourite names or something with an international flavour. Thus, in

La Realidad we found a Clinton and Floriberta and even Donaldo. Outside the forest, in the cold lands, the Tzeltal people from Oxchuc have two surnames from birth. The formal (Spanish) one, usually Morales, Santiz, Gómez, Méndez, López or Encino, and then the indigenous one, which varies but is related to the moment of birth or the pregnancy. For example, the position of the stars can determine the new-born's name. If the birth occurs in bright sunshine the child will be called 'K'aal', writes Martin Gómez Ramírez in *Offering to the Ancestors in Oxchuc*. Or if the mother dreams of an animal, plant or object during the pregnancy, this will be the paternal surname for the first born and those that follow. Gómez Ramírez points out:

'It is also said that right after the birth the parents examine the placenta carefully and patiently to see the shape and colour in the middle.'

There is a story of a man given the surname K'ulub, meaning locust, because when he was born the placenta was bright green. Gómez Ramírez also relates that:

If a man or a woman dreams of any part of the human body, let's say 'chinbak', which means knee, then that was the surname given to the new-born. However the Gómez of Oxchuc not only have 'k'ulub', but a relationship with plants, animals and other objects because they dreamt of them or imagined them...

Chapter 4

The women organise and become politically aware

It took many years of painstaking work to get indigenous women to participate in community life and even longer to involve them in Zapatista politics. It is an ongoing process and in many places in Chiapas women still don't count in public life. Nevertheless, a seed has been planted which is revolutionising the old ways and is already bearing fruit. The EZLN women's politicising work was patient and careful. Tzeltal Captain Maribel says that from the beginning 'our officers told us that we had to organise more *compañeras*'.

With this intention the rebel women came down from their mountain camps to approach the indigenous women in the towns. Even though they walked for several days, they were only able to visit three or four villages each time and had no guarantee of many women coming to meet them. Maribel explains that they tried to improve what they were doing.

- We started doing what we call radio-news programmes, covering a variety of topics. There might be an item on the struggle for land for example, explaining everything about the subject. Since not everyone in the communities understands Spanish, we do a translation. Some of the *compañeras* in the camp speak Tzotzil, others Tzeltal, others Tojolabal, so we would translate and record the news items, then send the tape to the communities. That's how the *compañeras* from the communities began to hear our political message. As time went by we started making inroads and the communities would invite us. They said 'please come, we want to meet you.'

That was during the time of gathering forces; the organisation was extremely secret and therefore any political undertaking had to be totally discreet.

- We rebel *compañeras* had to do this work whilst ensuring no one found out who we were or what we were doing. We invented pretexts, we said we were students or nuns preaching the Word of God. And actually we were, because the Word of God has to do with exploitation and injustice. The *compañeras* invited us so we went and talked with them about the national situation and why we have taken up arms. That was our work then. At the beginning it was hard, because many *compañeras* didn't read or write and we had to teach them and explain our political ideas to them in their dialect.

This consciousness-raising work was going on elsewhere too, as Ana María, a graceful Tzotzil with a *rebozo* (traditional shawl) thrown over her uniform, describes:

- What some of us do in the communities is set up women's groups and organise collectives. Those of us who have some education teach basic literacy to the *compañeras* from the villages. That's what we've being doing for many years.

Captain Laura, a Tzotzil by birth who has risen fast in rank, lost four brothers. She thinks she has eleven siblings still alive. When she was small she lived for a year in the city with her mother, while her father went to look for temporary work in the countryside. She went back to her community in Los Altos de Chiapas and as she had learned to read in San Cristóbal, she devoted herself to teaching other women in her collective, encouraged by her father.

- I was fourteen when my father began talking politics, about the situation in the country, of why we were poor, how women suffer... 'Look how you suffer,' he told me. I don't know how he knew, but one day he told me there was an armed struggle but no one should know. He asked me: 'What do you think?' I answered 'fine, but first let me work some more with the *compañeras*.' Laura and the others grew vegetables together. In the evenings after finishing their work, they would meet and she would recount her conversations with her father. As time went by, the talks became weekly and the women began to think for themselves.

- The women would be very anti-men. They said: 'men don't help us, we have to look after the children, your child can be crying and the men just ask for their dinner'. We had long discussions, about twenty of us - a very small community.

When Laura was fifteen, she entered the Zapatista militia, a halfway-house between life in the community and full army discipline. In this way she was able to join the struggle without leaving the village or the women's group. From then on she had to go to other communities to widen her knowledge and meet other groups of *compañeras* and see how they worked. She taught Spanish and learnt 'many things'. They helped her buy a collective sewing machine for her community.

- Many *compañeras* were already sharing our discussions with their husbands... As a result they started helping women in the house: 'If you want to stop exploitation then help me with the kids, the wood and the water.'

What the women in the villages thought of the Zapatista women

After joining up, Ana María made frequent visits to the women in the communities. Obviously it was a cultural shock for the indigenous women to accept one of them being totally involved in the armed struggle. Ana María, a Tzotzil, had abandoned the traditional dress, the weaving and children to take up a rifle alongside men. Surely it didn't look good to many of them. Ana María disagrees:

- No, quite the contrary, they thought it was fine. And many, many women wanted to join the struggle but they couldn't because they were already married and had children who they couldn't leave. But because we don't fight only with guns, women in the villages get organised, do collective work, set up study groups, learn from books. And they help the Zapatista Army, because the army is their children, their brothers, brothers in-law... They make sure they have food in the mountains.

Things were different for Irma, a twenty-eight year old captain.

- My friends said that I shouldn't go and that it isn't good for women to go... In the community we women couldn't express our opinion or participate in meetings, we were not taken into account... If I were still at home I would be bound to a man, who might be hitting and ill-treating me. Today in the communities the women often run away with their *compañero* because they don't want to be sold off by their fathers.

In the valley - more a gully, really - where the Tojolabal people live, Maribel explains that at the beginning it wasn't well thought of for a woman to become a guerrilla.

- There were many rumours about women in the mountains living with men... But we knew very well it wasn't like that because we were the ones experiencing it. Our relationship with the *compañeros* in the EZLN is based on help, companionship and respect; but you don't know that if you don't live in the group. That's what they thought outside, but at that time many *compañeras* in the communities were waiting for us to say 'if you want to come, then do it.'

The girls wanted to know how women could endure such a hard life in the mountains. So they asked rebels like Maribel.

- Just explain what you women do, we know there are many problems. What do you do when you are menstruating, for example? You don't walk, don't run, don't march? And the training? They thought of all those problems. And we told them that there's no suffering as bitter as that of the people. There's no comparison for someone who is aware of the situation, who has decided to fight. Personally, it isn't so bad. You get used to it. Then the *compañeras* said, 'Actually I want to be like you'. So that's how many joined. Almost a third of the EZLN are women.

- That's how we started making inroads, it was need which forced us. Our political understanding showed us that not only men are exploited, but also women. So if women are exploited they have the right and the duty to struggle for a more just society. That's what we understood, what I understood: we have to fight here, side by side with the *compañeros*, with weapons, supporting them somehow.

Maribel returns to the story of how the Zapatista women entered the villages to bring more women to the cause:

- We gathered the *compañeras* in groups and told them: we are fighting because we have to do something before we starve to death or die of some bloody disease. If we work in the health service for

69

example, when we go to give our political lessons, we talk about health and how to prevent illness, given that there aren't enough medicines or doctors in the communities.

They encouraged the women to join up.

- We wanted the *compañeras* to learn to work collectively as that would help them a lot. Slowly, the indigenous women began to get organised. There were many obstacles, of course, because they had never done such a thing before. We gave them some theoretical explanations first. Then they continued on their own; but if they had problems then they sent us a letter or sent someone with a message.

In Guadalupe Tepeyac, late in 1994, the women opened a collective restaurant for the many visitors and journalists in the area. They had realised that the visitors were asking for food in the houses near the hospital and therefore only a few families were benefiting from the visitors. The problem was solved in an assembly. The Guadalupe women decided it wasn't fair that some of them were getting rich and others weren't. So they decided to open a little collective restaurant in the space in front of the hospital which was re-christened the Che Guevara-Emiliano Zapata. They established shifts and the profits went to the collective. They set up a little warehouse; they also had a firewood oven nearby, built of clay and cement. They baked bread once a week, with flour and sugar which arrived by truck and was stored in the warehouse until Tuesday or Thursday, when they all gathered together to knead dough for bread and cakes. After it was baked they distributed their produce so every family in town could have some.

The women were satisfied:

- Collective work is much better because it brings us together and then no one can separate us, because our thinking is reflected in our actions and our actions reflect our thinking.

On 9 February 1995, faced with the military offensive, the community of Guadalupe Tepeyac embarked on an exodus, leaving behind everything they had built. But that was much later. Ten years ago, when the rebels were organising the women, the Indigenous Clandestine Revolutionary Committee was being set up. There were people in charge of working with the villages, wider rural areas and

70

the regions. These Committees took charge of the consciousness-raising work and slowly the rebels stopped appearing in the communities, unless they were asked to by the people. Maribel explains:

- Sometimes the Committee would say: 'the *compañeras* want you personally'. So we go, but it's at the Committee's request.... Recruitment was very slow because it was done family by family. A family in the community begins to participate in the EZLN. When there is a group in the village, they designate their local representative, but we ask them to choose not only from the men, but also from the *compañeras*. When we go there to talk to everyone we also talk to the *compañeras* alone. From then on the regions began to expand and regional representatives were selected and are the ones who make up the Committee.

Women start to speak

Major Ana María makes no bones about how difficult it was to get women involved.

- We insisted that the women also had to be organised. We told the *compañeras* they had to represent something, do something, not only the men. Whenever we went to the communities we found only men in the meetings or study circles. We put a lot of effort into getting the women to stand up and get the chance to do something. In the end they asked for themselves. They said: 'if the men are going to study and learn things, why not us? We want to be trained, we want to learn... Besides, we have *compañeras* who are rebels and they are showing they can do it. Women can, so give us a chance.'

From these beginnings the EZLN Revolutionary Law on Women started to develop. Maribel tells us what happened:

- When the discussion about revolutionary laws for women began, the *compañeras* were already aware of what they were fighting for and what their needs were, beyond the general demands of all people. The *compañeras* said: 'well, we can see that here in the villages there is injustice. The men think like the rich and they want to dominate women. This is not good for us. So then we started not just

71

organising women from one community but doing cultural events with several communities which the *compañeras* attended: mainly on the 8th of March - International Women's Day. The *compañeros* really tried to please us that day. The organisation was done jointly with the Youth Group. We had also started organising the younger people, from fifteen to thirty years old. Beyond thirty is considered too old.

- When we did women's events we brought the Youth Group so the *compañeras* could see what the youngsters, who are their children of course, were doing. Afterwards, the *compañeras'* representatives stepped up onto the stage one by one to say what they thought about the struggle, why they were fighting and also gave their opinion of the work, collectively, regionally or locally. As they got more involved, they began to develop political leadership. At that point they would say: 'now we need to make the decisions, like how many children we are going to have. We want to participate more in the struggle, be leaders, get the same money...'

- We had talked to them about the labour of workers and *campesinos* and said that there were some women workers in factories and they were paid less than the men. The same happens in the *fincas*, where women work cutting or sorting coffee. Because they are women sometimes they get no pay or less than men. The women said that it shouldn't be like that, that there has to be justice. And that's when the women's revolutionary laws are created. It wasn't us rebel women who wrote those laws. It was the *compañeras* in the indigenous communities. We were in some of their meetings because many of them don't understand Spanish and we had to translate for them, and would co-ordinate. We put together all of their demands. Not only from the *compañeras* from one village of region, but from all over.

- Each place drew up a draft, then all the versions were attached and sent back to each community. Then we explained to them, 'listen, we collected the opinions from all the *compañeras* and here are the laws...' And we explained to them, along with the Committee, what each law meant. And they said 'no, you have to take that out, because it isn't good for us... or we have to have this in too...' They studied it again and deleted what they disagreed with and sent it back again and it came back to them, and that's how the law was established.

The EZLN Women's Revolutionary Law

1. Women, whatever their race, creed or political affiliation, have the right to participate in the revolutionary struggle in accordance with their own will and ability.

2. Women have the right to work and be paid a fair salary.

3. Women have the right to decide the number of children they want to have and look after.

4. Women have the right to participate in community affairs and hold posts if freely and democratically elected.

5. Women and their children have the right to primary health care and food.

6. Women have the right to education.

7. Women have the right to choose their partner and not be forced into an arranged marriage.

8. No woman shall be beaten or physically abused by her family or strangers. Offences of attempted rape or rape will be severely punished.

9. Women can hold political and military leadership positions.

10. Women have all rights and obligations bestowed by the revolutionary laws and regulations.

'Now we see that there are other *compañeras* around the country who are in a different situation from those who live in the forest,' adds Maribel. 'Which is why we think those other women can add something to the Revolutionary Law because we want it to embrace the demands of all Mexican women. Obviously other women, for example, nurses, doctors, teachers, workers must all have their own demands that need to be taken into account.'

The adoption of the law

In the view of Subcomandante Marcos:

- The most ancient traditions of collective working, that is, not for personal benefit, comes from women. That group experience helped them to a better understanding of our cause. It explains the steely reply of the *campesinas*: 'yes, we are Zapatistas', even when they are under fire or near tanks.

In Marcos' view, the first EZLN uprising was 8 March 1993, when the women demanded the adoption of their revolutionary laws:

- That was quite something! Comandantes Ramona and Susana went to every community. Ramona went to the Tzotzil area, which is more close-minded and where the women are more isolated than in the Tzeltal area, where they are more open-minded. Tzotzil women don't talk to men. But Ramona spoke, she organised the communities and appointed women to lead the women's committees. When the war was voted for, they said: 'Well, we vote for war, but we'll make our own laws. Let's make our own laws.'

On that 8 March 1993 we were up in Los Altos in a committee meeting and it was terrible, all the women were wound up and if you were a man you felt like you were in trouble. When the women's law was read out, everyone started to comment. The Tzeltal men told their *compañeros* not to tell anyone about what they were discussing because it was going to be chaos.

Even better than in the previous interview, Marcos describes how that 'first uprising' occurred in a letter to journalist Alvaro Cepeda Neri (*La Jornada*, 30 January 1994):

Tzotzil Susana is angry. People had been making fun of her because she was blamed for the first EZLN uprising in March 1993. 'I'm furious', she tells me. I hide behind a rock until I find out why. 'The *compañeros* say that the Zapatistas' uprising last year was because of me.' I approach her cautiously. Then I find out what it's all about: in March 1993 the *compañeros* were discussing what would become the 'Revolutionary Laws'. Susana had to go to dozens of communities to talk to women's groups and distil their thinking into the 'Laws on Women'. The CCRI met to vote for the laws and to listen to the opinion of the different committees - justice, land, war taxes, rights and responsibilities of the people in struggle, and women. Susana had to read the proposals she had collected from the ideas of thousands of indigenous women. She began to read and as she did so the assembly became increasingly restless. Whispers and comments began to be heard. In Chol, Tzotzil, Tzeltal, Tojolabal, Mam, Zoque and 'Castillian', comments bounced to and fro. Susana continued, although she was fuming:

- We don't want to be obliged to marry against our will. We want to have the number of children we choose and can look after. We want the right to hold positions in the community. We want the right to express our opinions and be respected. We want the right to study and even be drivers.' By the time she concluded she was met by a palpable silence. The laws for women Susana had just read were a revolution for the indigenous communities. The men were looking nervously at each other. Suddenly, almost simultaneously, the translators finished and in a swelling movement the *compañeras* started to clap. The laws for women were of course approved unanimously.

- One Tzeltal leader commented: 'It's a good thing my wife doesn't speak Spanish, otherwise...' A Tzotzil major of infantry threw herself at him: 'You're out of luck, you fool, we're going to translate it into all the dialects'. The *compañero* lowered his gaze. The women are singing, the men scratching their heads, bewildered.

I decided it would be prudent to call a break.

So the first EZLN uprising was in March 1993 and it was led by the Zapatista women. There were no casualties - they won. These are the things that happen around here!

Tzotzil Major Ana María has another version.

- We protested because there was no law for women. And that's how it was born; we made it and presented it at an assembly of everyone, men and women, representatives from the villages. One *compañera* read it and no one argued, everyone agreed, it was voted on, no problem.

- The law was written by some of the women asking the *compañeras* for their opinion, their desires and needs. Their opinions were collected in each village and then those of us who can write wrote it down.

To Subcomandante Marcos, this law is a real revolution of tradition.

- To differing degrees women are marginalised in every ethnic group, but what was approved in the women's laws was virtually unthinkable in many places where couples that don't have permission are sent to jail or tied to a post on a basket-ball court until they pay for their sin. There is buying and selling of women; food or alcohol is given in exchange for a girl and some run away from their communities because they can't afford to pay the bill.

The Zapatista military leader recounts a case that took place after the adoption of the law.

- A couple were going out and were caught by the community and jailed. She defended herself and told them: 'No one can lock me up, you voted for those laws, so I have the right to sleep with whoever I want'. She faced the community assembly and they had to set her free because she told them 'what's a law for if it can't be applied?'. Since the land law was at stake, they accepted because they thought the war compensation wouldn't be applied either. She was released because she was a delegate from the Indigenous Clandestine Revolutionary Committee and she knew the law; otherwise they would have tied her up.

A profound change

Maribel says:

- Before the EZLN, the *compañeras* were beaten up, they were obliged to marry someone they didn't love, there was a lot of drunkenness and that also hurt the *compañeras*, because they were always crying and having to protect themselves from their husbands' machetes...

- When we came here we made a law forbidding alcohol, because you can't have people getting drunk and then giving us away.

- It was agreed it had to be that way, because such evil vices bring trouble to the family and the community. But since things have changed the communities are more peaceful.

Nevertheless, the men in the indigenous villages had trouble accepting the women's new role, their demands and their participation. Maribel explains:

- The *compañeros* saw these changes and the women's political training in the communities. They had problems because the *compañera* could now stand up for herself: 'I am going to the meeting and I will go because we agreed on that with the other women'.

- So now our duty is to participate in the assemblies and discuss the community's problems. So the few *compañeros* who made trouble were overruled by the other *compañeros* and by the women themselves. And finally now, the revolutionary law really is being implemented. Men do miss the past, because now they can't just beat up their wives, they can't make us marry someone our father wants; if a woman doesn't love a man, well, she doesn't love him. Now a woman can take legal action against her husband and tell the authorities: 'look at what is happening ... or 'he is hitting me...' They can speak out and denounce something. And that's why sometimes men are imprisoned, sometimes they have to go and work as punishment for assaulting a women or attempted rape or constant beatings or not getting along. But the conflict doesn't stay just in the family, it is solved positively with the authorities.

- A woman couldn't do that before, as soon as she goes to complain, her husband beats her harder, he gets more pissed off. Not anymore; now she says: 'you are going to behave or I'll leave.' And she does.

- If the man wants her back, he looks for her and starts over. But there's the feeling that he has to mend his ways. I've witnessed some of these cases being resolved that way.

- The relationship of a couple in the communities is very hard. A separated woman isn't alone, she has her two or three children. So they have to reach an agreement. 'If you're leaving me you take this one and I'll take that one.' But it occurs under the eyes of the whole community.

- You learn to solve problems according to the revolutionary law. So now the *compañeras* have some defence. And that defence makes them strong, so that they won't allow themselves to be humiliated any more.

- There has been a change, but for some *compañeros* it is a bit difficult because traditions don't disappear in two or three days: it takes months and years.

Women s day in the Lacandon forest

The date is the 8th March 1994. A member of the Indigenous Clandestine Revolutionary Committee in a balaclava speaks. The dark night shields the Zapatista people from the eagle eye of the military aeroplanes. About four hundred rebels gathered in the square, two lines, men and women face to face, surrounded by children and the other community residents, all listening attentively.

- *Compañeros* and *compañeras*, in the name of the General Command of the Zapatista Army I'm going to read some words. Today, 8th of March, let's honour those women who, long ago in an American factory, organised to fight for women's rights. All our women must follow their example, for women are also able to pay the price of involvement in a real cause.

- Today we bring fraternal and revolutionary greetings to all the *compañeras* in our rebel and militia ranks and to all the women in our villages...The idea that women are good only for the home and raising children or for the bourgeoisie to have cheap labour is not for us. The 'enough is enough!' of the 1st of January must reach to the remotest place, to wherever there is one of our women.

These were the words of the meeting co-ordinator, a man, on that 8th of March in the Ocosingo gully. After him Captain Irma read her speech:

- Dear *compañeros* and *compañeras*. We are gathered here to celebrate the 8th of March, Women's International Day, for those women who have given their lives to defend their rights, who worked in bad conditions and without pay and decided to rise up in struggle [...] That's why now I invite all the *compañeras*, from the countryside and the city, to support our demands, for women are the most exploited of all.

- Most women can't even read and write because men want to keep them downtrodden. *Compañeras*, wherever you are, in order to stop this we have to fight along with the *compañeros* in our army to make ourselves understood. Women too can fight with guns. I invite you to support us in what we ask as Zapatistas. I know it is difficult, but we have to fight until we win or die, there's no other way, they haven't left us any other option. We will continue our struggle until we get what we are asking for: bread, democracy, peace, independence, justice, freedom, housing, health, because the poor don't have any of those things. That's why we are trapped, because we can't read, sometimes many of us don't know what the masters are telling us even if they are telling us off, we think they are saying good things. It suits them that we don't know how to write, because it's easier for the bastards to use us.

- We have had enough, we don't want to live like animals any longer, always being told what to do or not do. Today more than ever we have to fight together so that one day we will be free. We'll win sooner or later; we will, that's for sure. Let's keep going - that's all I have to say. Thank you.

After that the singing began. The sky was star-spangled, the darkness violated only by the irritating light of the journalists' video cameras and the photographers' flashes. Shyly, softly, slightly out of tune, the rebel women sang the Latin American Hymn of the Women of the Earth.

'Forward, women of the earth/ let's fight for liberation/ united against imperialism/ united by the revolution.'

Men were in charge of organising the party. They killed, cleaned and cooked several pigs. They were also in charge of lighting the fire, making the *tortillas*, coffee and rice. Subcomandante Marcos, in one of his poetic moments, ordered them to pick and arrange some wild flowers, but the forest heat soon turned them into bunches of wilted leaves.

The 'Sub' made the rebel men line up in front of the women combatants. Solemnly he said: 'the *compañeros* are going to give a rebel salute to the *compañeras* for International Women's Day.'

The party continued. The village women, their children in their arms or playing around them, listened attentively to the rebel women's speeches. The contrast between them is enormous: the indigenous women dressed in traditional dresses with coloured ribbons, barefoot, slender, condemned to maternity, to the kitchen, to neither understand nor speak Spanish. And then the rebels, daughters or sisters or friends or neighbours of these same women. The Zapatistas are better nourished so their bodies are filled out, they wear military boots, trousers and uniform, they carry a weapon. More than that, they are bold, fearless, self-confident despite their youth. They not only speak Spanish but are not ashamed to read their own speeches aloud in front of everyone. Of course, there had to be dancing. A sound system plugged into a car battery amplified favourite records. With the very first chord of the first *cumbia,* the single girls from the village flooded the dance floor, dancing together. The young men joined them, but they never dance close or look into each other's eyes. Another very widespread tradition is that married or engaged women can't dance.

Since the beginning of the war, many city women from the civil organisations have come to these places. The girls from the international peace convoys or from the civil peace camps (set up after the military incursion in February 1995) dance, even if they're engaged, swapping partners and encouraging the others to do so. The younger indigenous folk are digesting these novelties, growing up seeing the contrast between the rebels and outsiders and their own selfless mothers. There won't be much space to follow a tradition that had appeared to be set in stone. Dances in the Tzeltal gully or the Tojolabal area in the Lacandon forest are similar. The rebel boys hurry to ask the girls to dance, the women watching, men from the Clandestine Committee politely ask the foreigners to dance and the rebels dance with each other. In the Tzeltal area, where there are more women warriors than in the Tojolabal area, they laugh, talk, approach their *compañeros*, chase and court them. I remember Captain Irma setting out to win Major Rolando; both wearing balaclavas, joking and laughing, dancing together, gazing into each other's eyes, weapons touching.

So many dances took place in those thirteen months of 'liberated' territory in the Lacandon forest (from January 1994 to February 1995)! The same scene of union between Zapatistas and the people, brown shirts with weapons dancing with pink dresses with coloured ribbons, brown shirts and caps with brown shirts with braids or pony-tails... And weapons, weapons, more weapons. In every conceivable combination. Azucena, who holds the rank of private, walks arm-in-arm with Captain Martín. Despite their happy smiles, and to my disappointment, they divorce two months later.

The heroic deeds of the Zapatista women

Subcomandante Marcos recounts:

- Our women are very brave. In Ocosingo, when some *compañeros* got stuck in the market because of the federal army bombing, it was a wounded *compañera* who took command and organised the resistance. She was a lower-ranking officer than the one in charge of the operation, who didn't know what to do.

He was speaking of Isidora. I found her in the Ocosingo gully, acting as one of the subcomandante's personal guards, riding a horse proudly. She had already recovered from the shrapnel which had scraped her spinal cord. In April 1994 Isidora was about twenty years old. All the journalists agreed she was beautiful; her mask couldn't hide the beauty of her almost oriental, almond-shaped eyes. She was wearing her hair in a pony-tail under her brown cap. A true Amazon, her personality fitting her warrior image, silent and tough. Her life story partly explains her implacable decision to challenge death and take up a gun. Conditions in her village were bad, there was no teacher or school. She helped her mother at home. But they had no land. Who knows why, but she says one day government people

81

came to her town and set all the houses on fire. 'They threw us out and we were left with nothing.' So they went to Ocosingo and lived there for two years, after which they decided to go back to the forest. 'We went deep into the mountains, settled in a small village and stayed.'

Upon finding out about the EZLN, she didn't think twice. Her parents supported her decision. She is the only one of her brothers and sisters who decided to become an insurgent. Isidora says her family is more relaxed now that she is in the EZLN, maybe it's because at least she has something to eat. Isidora never thought she was going to be the heroine of Ocosingo. Interviewed, she was brief:

- The soldiers arrived in the afternoon of the 2nd of January. We were in the market, when Major Mario told us the army were coming. Captain Benito, who lost an eye to shrapnel that day, told us we couldn't abandon our positions until we got instructions from our HQ. More than twenty trucks loaded with soldiers came. We started shooting; I was on the front line, in charge of forty militia members. We were told that Captain Benito and Captain Elsa were hurt. So I stood there on my own, with no commanding officer, and had to take control of my troops. At nine at night there were only wounded left. I didn't know what to do, the grenade splinters had hurt my back and my wrist and a bullet had grazed my foot. But at least I could drag myself, if not walk. And dragging myself I had to take out all the wounded, as best I could. I kept telling myself: 'as long as I'm alive I'll get them out, if they stay here they'll be killed'. More than thirty wounded made it, some walking. We left only the dead behind in the market square, some four *compas*. Some civilians died too, because the soldiers were firing all over the place. There was a helluva lot of them and so few of us because most of our forces had already fallen back. We were only about ten insurgents, the rest were militia and they don't have decent weapons, they have 22 calibre rifles or air-rifles.

- It was two in the morning and we crossed a field to move towards the road. Dawn came and I didn't know what to do or where the rest of the *compañeros* were. I couldn't move because my wounds had swollen. I thought I was going to die. But the *compas* found us.

Ana María holds a high rank in the EZLN: she was in charge of the occupation of San Cristóbal on the 1st of January 1994.

- We voted to begin the war. Then we started preparing the strategy. I command a unit and of course I had to be at the front to be an example to the *compañeros*. We are organised in units. I command a big unit which includes a lot of militia members, more than a thousand. Inside the unit we are divided into smaller units, each with its own comandante. Each comandante receives instructions, he is told how to attack and each one knows what has to be done. When we took over San Cristóbal some had patrol posts, some set the ambush, others were back-up at the entry/exit points. Each unit had a mission to accomplish. Others went into the Office of the Presidency. On the day after the attack on the Cereso prison, it was women who broke in and opened the doors to free the inmates.

Captain Maribel was assigned to take over Las Margaritas' radio station. She recounts:

- Since I hold military rank I was clear what I had to do on the day. We concentrated the troops in one place and left for Las Margaritas. Everyone knew what they had to do, although we didn't know the city. I had only been once and didn't know where I was going. The first mistake we made was passing in front of the Office of the Presidency in an open vehicle, with all the *compañeros* sitting inside. The police there just stared at us. But just a block away we got a flat tyre. So I decided everyone should get out and run the few blocks left. It was pretty far from where we had to go.

- I had to appoint another group to go and get us a car in case we were ordered to withdraw. So that's when the shooting began at the Presidency. They didn't shoot at us, but the attacking forces had already reached the Presidency. My main objective was to ask the people in the radio station to do us the favour of playing a tape to broadcast our struggle to the whole region. But it wasn't possible because there was nobody there, they were celebrating New Year with their families. We took over the station and stayed until we were ordered to withdraw. I left the tape, because I had to leave, so other *compañeros* played it.

- On the second day my mission was removing weapons from the land-owners. I organised my forces again, as ordered, and we began taking over the farms. We recovered the weapons they had there, guns and larger calibre rifles and grenades.

- Someone from a farm had fired at a group of *compañeros* before we started the war, because he found out they were Zapatistas. They weren't allowed to take anything with them, they were chased away and shot at and had grenades thrown at them. At that time our officers said there was nothing we could do, it was better to leave, stay in town until we started the war and then recover the weapons.

- So we did. The owner of the farm wasn't there but someone else was in charge. We surrounded the place and told him to give us the weapons. He said no, that he didn't have any. We told him we were coming in to check. We did and there they were, he didn't want to give them to us.

- The next day I went back with the *compañeros* who had been sacked the year before. They hadn't been able to collect their things since then - their clothes, beds, houses, nothing. So I went with them and asked them: 'well, what is it you left here?' 'Well this is my hen, that is my bed, that is my house.' 'Now it's yours' I said. And that is how we started carrying out that sort of mission, not only there but further afield.

'We won't stop this struggle until our demands are fulfilled,' says Maribel forcefully. As regards the future and what she would like to be or do, she says:

- It all depends, it will be whatever the people ask of me. If the people say 'we don't need you as a soldier any more', I can always get some other job that will be useful to me and to the people.

Laura is a captain also. She acquired her rank after she passed her exams, like all the captains, before the members of the Indigenous Clandestine Revolutionary Committee. Laura was in charge of the most difficult battle of all, the occupation of Ocosingo. Laura tells us how she felt before leaving the forest for the city.

- You are nervous, but you are conscious that at the same time you have to stay in control. I had eighty militia and four insurgents under my command. When you are the captain you have to be able to encourage and lead people, and you must be at the front.

She says she only had one thing on her mind:

- You want to get it right. To watch a soldier fall is a terrible sight. I'm going to shoot but I can't miss, I can't miss a shot, that's what you have in mind. And commanding your people, encouraging them: 'aim and shoot: now!'

Laura doesn't make any predictions about what will happen. She is pragmatic, holds tight to her weapon, which she says is an extension of her body. Asked what she would like to do or be in a hypothetical peaceful future, she replies:

- I will continue in the army, it's the only thing I know how to do. I like reading and studying, but... besides, when you win a war you keep the taste of war, don't you? You want to continue as before, what you learnt to be. And that is what I like to be because my gun is like a part of my own body.

Laura's stark reply raises more questions. What happens when this is over? What chances are there for these young girl soldiers to fit back into society, into that distant daily reality of their birthplace?

Marcos writes about the insurgent women
Twelve women in the twelfth year (the second of war)

In the EZLN's twelfth year, far away, thousands of miles from Beijing, twelve women approach the 8th of March 1996 with their faces hidden.

I. Yesterday

From behind the black mask only the eyes and a few hairs peep out. The eyes shine as they search. An M-1 carbine is slung in front, in the 'assault' position, and a pistol hangs at the waist. Over the left breast, the place of hope and conviction, the Major of Infantry insignia of an insurgent army that had called itself, up until that cold dawn on the 1st of January 1994, the Zapatista Army for National Liberation. Under her command is the rebel column which takes the ancient capital of the south-eastern Mexican state of Chiapas, San Cristóbal de Las Casas. San Cristóbal's central square is deserted.

Only the indigenous men and women under her command witness the moment in which the Major, a woman, a Tzotzil Indian and a rebel, picks up the national flag and gives it to the Indigenous Clandestine Revolutionary Committee. On the radio, the Major communicates: 'we recovered the flag. 10-23, waiting.' She waited for ten years to say those seven words. She arrived in the Lacandon mountains in December 1984, not yet twenty years old, but with the history of the humiliation of the Indian peoples on her shoulders. In December 1984 this woman said 'Enough is enough!', but she said it so softly only she could hear it.

In January 1994, this woman and tens of thousands of indigenous people shouted 'Enough is enough!'; they say it so loud the whole world can hear them... In the outskirts of San Cristóbal another rebel column is commanded by a man. He is the only one with white skin and a big nose among the Indians taking the city, and has just finished attacking the police headquarters. From the clandestine jails they release the Indians spending New Year locked up for the worst offence in the Southeast of Chiapas: being poor. The Captain's name is Eugenio Asparuk, he is a Tzeltal Indian and commands the search of the police headquarters. When the Major's message comes through, Chol Captain Pedro has successfully captured the headquarters of the Federal Transport Police and has command of the San Cristóbal - Tuxtla Gutiérrez highway. Tzeltal Captain Ubilio has control of the northern access to the city and occupies the symbol of the government's paltry offering to the indigenous people: the National Indigenous Institute. Captain Guillermo, another Chol, has control of the high point of the city, from where he dominates the surprised silence almost visible in the windows of the buildings below him. Captains Gilberto and Noe, Tzotzil and Tzeltal respectively, wind up the assault on the State Judicial Police headquarters, set it on fire, and go to secure the edge of the city that communicates with the 31st Military Zone headquarters in Rancho Nuevo.

Five male indigenous insurgent officers listen on the radio to their woman comandante's voice saying 'we recovered the flag, 10-23 waiting.' They repeat and translate it to their troops: 'we've begun...'

In the Town Hall, the Major organises the defence of the position and protection for those men and women who have control of the city, all indigenous rebels. An armed woman protects them.

Among the rebellion's indigenous leaders there's a tiny woman. Her face is also masked in black, showing but her eyes and some hair on her neck. A 12 calibre sawn-off shotgun hangs from her shoulder. Wearing the traditional costume of the people of San Andrés, Ramona comes down from the mountains, along with hundreds of women, towards the city of San Cristóbal, on the last night of 1993. Together with Susana and the others, she is part of the indigenous war command at the dawn of 1994: the EZLN's Indigenous General Command Clandestine Revolutionary Committee. At the Dialogue in the Cathedral Comandante Ramona will shine for the international media, both because of her diminutive stature and her strategic brilliance. In her haversack she carries the national flag the Major recovered on the 1st of January. At that time Ramona did not know, and neither did we, that she carries in her body a disease that is eating away at her, dimming her voice and sight. Ramona and the Major, the only women in the Zapatista delegation, seen for the first time in the Dialogue, declare: 'we were dead already, we didn't count for anything', and they say it as if they were drawing up a balance-sheet of humiliation and oblivion. The Major translates the journalists' questions for Ramona. She nods in understanding, as if the answer requested were obvious. She laughs at the Spanish and the city women's way of being. Ramona laughs before she knows she is dying. When she finds out, she's still laughing. Before she didn't exist for anyone, now she does, she is a woman, indigenous and rebellious.

The Major watches the daylight stealing through the streets of San Cristóbal. Her soldiers organise the defence of the ancient Jovel area and protection for the men and women still asleep. Whatever their ethnicity they will all be amazed. This indigenous woman Major has occupied the city for them. Hundreds of armed Indians surround the ancient Royal City. An armed woman commands them...

Minutes later the county town of Las Margaritas falls into rebel hands, hours later the government forces defending Ocosingo, Altamirano and Chanal surrender. Huixtan and Oxchuch are taken by a column going towards the main jail in San Cristóbal. Seven of the county towns are under rebel control after the Major's fateful seven words. The war of words has begun...

Irma. Insurgent Captain of Infantry, a Chol Indian, leads one of the guerrilla columns that take Ocosingo square on the 1st of January 1994. From the side of the central square her troops have hounded the garrison guarding the Town Hall until they surrender. Then Irma loosens her hair from its braid and it falls free to her waist, as though saying 'here I am, free and new.' Captain Irma's hair shines until night falls over rebel-held Ocosingo...

Laura. Insurgent Captain of Infantry, a Tzotzil woman, courageous in fighting and studying. Laura became Captain of a male-only unit. Not only are they all men, they are new recruits. Patiently, like the mountain that watched her grow, Laura teaches and commands. When the men under her command hesitate, she sets the example. No one in her unit carries or walks as much as her. After the attack on Ocosingo, she withdraws her unit, complete and in order. This woman makes no idle boast, but she carries the carbine she took from a policeman. After surrendering, the policeman ran away wearing no more than his underpants. Until that day, he thought women were only useful for cooking and producing children...

Silvia. Insurgent Captain of Infantry. She spent ten days in the death-trap that was Ocosingo after the 2nd of January. Dressed in civilian clothes she escapes through the streets full of federal soldiers, tanks and cannons. A military patrol stops her. They let her through almost immediately. 'How could such a young delicate girl be a rebel?' say the soldiers watching her walk away. Joining her unit in the mountains again, Silvia looks sad. Carefully I ask her what saddens her. 'I left my rucksack with all the music tapes down in Ocosingo, so we don't have music anymore.' She hides her silence and sorrow between her hands. I keep silent in empathy, seeing that in war, everyone loses their most precious possession.

Maribel. Insurgent Captain of Infantry. She takes over Las

Margaritas' radio station when her unit occupies the main town of the municipality on the 1st of January 1994. Nine years of her life led to that moment when she sat in front of the microphone and said: 'we are the product of 500 hundred years of struggle: first against slavery...' The broadcast didn't take place because of technical problems and Maribel withdrew to cover the unit going towards Comitán. Days later she will have to escort the prisoner of war General Asalón Castellanos Dominguez. Maribel is a Tzeltal and she was barely fifteen years old when she arrived in the mountains of Chiapas. 'The most difficult moment in those nine years was when I had to climb up the first hill, the 'hill of hell', after that everything was a lot easier'. In releasing General Castellanos Dominguez, Captain Maribel is the first one to make contact with the government. Commissioner Manuel Camacho Solís shakes her hand and asks her age: '502' says Maribel, counting the years from when the rebellion started.

Isidora. Infantry soldier. Isidora enters Ocosingo on the 1st of January. She leaves Ocosingo in flames, it takes her hours to get her all-male unit out: forty are wounded. She also has grenade splinters in her arms and legs. Isidora gets to the health-post and delivers the wounded, asks for a little water and gets up. 'Where are you going?', they ask her when they try to heal her bleeding wounds. Blood covers her face and stains her uniform red. 'To get the others', she says loading cartridges. They try to stop her but can't. Private soldier Isidora insists she has to go back to Ocosingo to take more *compañeros* out of the deadly music the mortars and grenades are singing. They have to lock her up to stop her. 'The good thing is, if they punish me they can't lower my rank', says Isidora, waiting in the room used as her jail. Months later, when she is given the star promoting her to infantry officer, Isidora looks from the star to her officer and asks, unsure, 'why?' She doesn't wait for an answer...

Amalia. Health Division Deputy-Lieutenant. With the quickest laugh in the Mexican south-east, Amalia lifts Captain Benito out of the pool of blood in which he is lying unconscious and drags him to a safe place. She carries him out of the belt of death tightening around the market square. When someone talks of surrendering,

Amalia, honouring her Chol blood, gets angry and starts arguing. Everyone listens to her, despite the explosions and gunfire all about them. No one surrenders.

Elena, Health Division Lieutenant. Illiterate when she first came to the EZLN. There she learned how to read and write and to do what passes for nursing, that is, how to cure diarrhoea and vaccinate. From curing diarrhoea and vaccinating, Elena went on to cure war wounds in a little hospital which doubles up as home, warehouse and pharmacy. With difficulty she extracts mortar shrapnel from the bodies of the Zapatistas arriving at her health post. 'Some can be extracted, some can't', says Elena, a Chol insurgent, as if she were talking about memories and not pieces of lead... In San Cristóbal, in the morning of the 1st of January 1994, Elena communicates with the man with the light complexion and the big nose : 'Someone came asking questions, but I can't understand the language, it seems to be English. I don't know if he is a journalist, but he carries a camera.'

'I'm coming over there', he says and puts on his balaclava.

He loads a vehicle with the weapons they recovered at the police headquarters and makes his way towards the town centre. They unload the weapons and give them to the indigenous people guarding the Town Hall. The foreigner is a tourist asking if he can leave town. 'No', answers the big nose, 'you better go back to your hotel. We don't know what is going to happen'. The foreign tourist goes away after asking permission to take some video shots. In the meanwhile, morning is passing, onlookers, journalists and questions arrive. The big nose answers and explains to locals, tourists and journalists. The Major is behind him. The leader in his balaclava talks and jokes. An armed woman guards his back.

A television reporter behind his camera asks: 'Who are you?'

'Who am I?' hesitates the man behind the balaclava.

'Yes' the reporter insists.

'Are you 'Comandante Tiger' or 'Comandante Lion'?'

'Oh, no!' answers he, rubbing his eyes in annoyance.

'Then, what's your name?', asks the journalist closing in with camera and microphone.

The balaclava with the big nose answers: 'Marcos. Subcomandante Marcos...'

In the sky the Pilatus aeroplanes manoeuvre...

From then on the taking of San Cristóbal unfolds without a hitch. The fact that the commanding officer was a woman is forgotten. The participation of women combatants in other actions on 1st January and during the ten long years since the birth of the EZLN becomes less important. The faces behind the balaclavas are completely forgotten as the lenses focus on Marcos. The Major is silent, covering the back of the owner of that prominent nose which now has a name for the rest of the world. No one asks her name.

On the early morning of the 2nd January 1994 this woman leads the withdrawal from San Cristóbal towards the mountains. She goes back to San Cristóbal fifty days later, part of the escort of the EZLN's delegates to the Dialogue at the Cathedral. Some women journalists interview her and ask her name. 'Ana María, Insurgent Major Ana María', she answers, regarding them from her dark eyes. She leaves the Cathedral and disappears for the rest of 1994. Like her other *compañeras*, she has to wait, silently...

In December 1994, ten years after becoming a soldier, Ana María receives the order to prepare to break through the government forces' siege of the Lacandon forest. In the early hours of 19 December the EZLN takes possession of thirty-eight municipalities. Ana María commands the action in the municipalities of Los Altos de Chiapas. Twelve women officers are with her in action: Monica, Isabela, Yuri, Patricia, Juana, Ofelia, Celina, María, Gabriela, Alicia, Zenaida and María Luisa. Ana María herself takes the county town of Bochil.

After the Zapatista withdrawal, the federal army high command orders that nothing should be said about the siege being broken and that the media should treat it as merely an EZLN propaganda action. Federal pride was hurt twice: the Zapatistas broke through the siege and worse, a woman was commanding the unit that took several of the main towns in the municipality. Quite impossible to accept, so a lot of money has to be invested in keeping it quiet from the public.

Firstly as a result of their companion-in-arms' thoughtlessness, secondly from the deliberate action of the government, Ana María and the Zapatista women with her are minimised, made smaller...

II. Today...

She. She holds no military rank, nor wears uniform, nor carries weapons. She is Zapatista but only she knows. Like the Zapatista women she is faceless and nameless. She fights for democracy, freedom, justice. She is part of what the EZLN calls 'civil society', people without a party, people who don't belong to the 'political society' of government and political party leaders. She is part of that uncharted but real entity, that part of society that every day says 'enough is enough!' She has also said 'enough is enough!' At the beginning she amazed herself with those words, but after repeating them and especially after living them, she stopped being afraid of them or afraid of herself. Now she is a Zapatista and is part of an outpouring of support for the Zapatista National Liberation Front, to the horror of political parties and establishment intellectuals alike. She has already fought against everybody, against her husband, her lover, her boyfriend, her children, her brother, her father, her grandfather. 'You're crazy' was the unanimous verdict. What she leaves behind is not inconsequential. What she is giving up, if we were talking in terms of quantity, is more than that of those rebels who have nothing to lose. Everything in her world demands she forget those 'crazy Zapatistas' and conformity calls her to the comfortable indifference of those who only look after themselves. She leaves everything. She doesn't say a thing. Early in the morning she sharpens the young blade of hope and emulates her Zapatista sisters' first of January several times in the same day. She smiles, she did admire the Zapatistas, but no longer. She stopped admiring them when she realised they were just a mirror of her own rebellion, of her own hope. She discovers she was born on the 1st of January 1994. She has felt alive since then: everything she was told was a dream, just utopia, can come true. Along with other men and women, expecting no reward, she starts silently weaving this complicated dream which some call hope: all for one and one for all.

She arrives on the 8th of March with her face and her name hidden. Along with her are thousands of women. More and more come. Dozens, hundreds, millions of women around the world reminded of how much there is still to do, how much to fight for.

Because it so happens that the thing about dignity is that it is contagious and women are very prone to catching this uncomfortable malady.

This 8th of March is a good pretext to acknowledge what the Zapatista women have done, with or without arms. And to remember the rebels and those other restless Mexican women determined to show that history, without them, is nothing but history gone awry...

III. Tomorrow...

If there is a tomorrow it will be with them and most of all, for them...

From the mountains of the Mexican Southeast,
Insurgent Subcomandante Marcos

The rebel women explain their ideas

- How many mothers have cried for their children, murdered, defending their rights and fighting for their brothers. How many mothers suffer the pain of their children being 'disappeared', how many mothers die in childbirth for lack of a doctor or medicine, how many mothers die for lack of food, how many women are mistreated, cheated with unfair wages, how many women are ill and malnourished, anaemic, how many women and their children suffer such injustice? How many imprisoned, murdered, tortured, missing women, because they fought for something better for the people, because they defended their rights and made demands, and fought against an evil government. How many widows or defenceless orphans suffer unjustly?

This is Captain Maribel's message to Mexican women at the National Consultation on Peace with Justice and Dignity.

- We rebel women don't care how much we must sacrifice to end these injustices. To us the greatest suffering is that of the Mexican people and our whole country. However, it not only causes us pain to see so much injustice, it also gives us the courage to fight; so here we are as insurgents, right beside our male *compañeros*. It was our evil government which obliged us to prepare and arm ourselves. Only then did they listen to us: now they listen but it is because of the work of you women, my sisters, around the country: we acknowledge your courage and your support.

In August 1995, the EZLN carried out a consultation on the organisation's future. For this unprecedented plebiscite, the insurgent women sent a message in an audio cassette calling all Mexican women to participate. A female voice explained:

- We, the Zapatista women said on the 1st of January 1994 'Enough is enough!' This evil government answers us with bombings, tanks and submachine guns. We have brothers who have fallen, mothers crying with the pain of their children's absence, because the only answer of that evil government was to launch a military offensive. But this blood spilt for us was not in vain because civil society has awoken and the evil government has listened to us.

The Zapatista leader called for more organisation:

- We women must fight to defend our rights and struggle to be listened to, respected... We are human beings too and part of society; we also have courage and strength, and with training can be leaders. We have the right, Mexican sisters, to fight for our rights, to terminate this terrible inequality, the awful injustice and exploitation we've been suffering for many years. That's why we have been divided in the past, because we have allowed bad leaders to do as they wish. We've suffered too much... We've seen our brothers killed by government bullets. Fighting for justice, freedom and democracy, they are beaten up, poisoned, tortured and murdered. Remember the massacre on the 2nd October 1968 when the blood of young students was spilt, and the continuous massacre of indigenous people all over the country, all over our Mexico. There is money for killing, money for munitions, money for troops.

- We are calling the mothers of the military to counsel their children wisely and tell them it is not right to die carrying out the orders of an evil government against the people. Tell them our mother country is for all Mexicans...

The message ends:

- We invite you to participate in the National Consultation on the 27th August 1995. We Zapatistas want to know what is in your hearts, your thoughts, sisters, so that we can better direct our fight for democracy, freedom and justice… To live for our homeland or to die for freedom!

A song dedicated to women goes like this:

Here I come to sing/ to my Mexican people,/ this is not a folk song/ nor a popular song,/ it is a call señores/ it is a call to fight./ This is no time to complain any more/ it is no time to cry,/ conscientious Mexicans/ willing to fight,/ have to get ready,/ get ready to fight. / Being a people's soldier,/ becoming an insurgent,/ isn't easy at all, señores,/ you have to be brave/ and say it with pride/ 'I want to be an insurgent'./ Today I've decided,/ this has to be finished,/ here I am *compañeros*,/ willing to fight,/ and that way live for the homeland/ or die for freedom.

Chapter 5

The Zapatista support base

The story of La Realidad

To get to La Realidad, literally 'Reality', you have to travel more than one hundred kilometres by dirt road into the heart of the forest. After Guadalupe Tepeyac the climb up the Cerro Quemado begins, and on the other side of the plains, lies this *ejido*. The mud, wood and straw houses, some of them with zinc sheeting, are set to the right and left of the road which cuts through in a straight line. A winding river brings fresh water to the huts. As in most villages of the area, each family has two huts, one for sleeping and one for the kitchen, the women's territory.

It was spring of 1995 when we first entered one of these kitchens. Ruth, a forty-two year-old Tojolabal, wears her hair braided down her back and, like all the women in the community, bright-coloured dresses, 'like a butterfly'. She is wearing a yellow dress with fluorescent green trimming, protected by a blue and white apron. This barefoot, strong-willed, beautiful, confident woman already has grandchildren although she only had two children. She has 'two families' she says.

We drink coffee from pewter mugs, sitting on wooden stools at a rickety table. The freshly-made *tortillas* are transferred from the comal to a calabash. We worship the piping-hot delicious coffee. Not to mention the *tortillas* which are made of 'real maize', hand-made, wonderfully tasty. Ruth smiles when we thank her, she is relaxed and happy with her visitors.

Jesus and Magdalena, both journalists, light up a cigarette and offer the others. Ruth comes closer and takes one from the proffered packet. She bends towards the flame of the lighter and lights up. She likes smoking, she expels the smoke at once and holds the cigarette with her thumb and index finger, in a sort of masculine way that contrasts with the femininity of her gestures and colourful appearance. This will be our first contact with the women of La Realidad, the female support base of the Zapatistas.

The soldiers stumbled into La Realidad

In February 1995 the federal army penetrated deep into the Lacandon forest. After seizing Guadalupe Tepeyac and Aguas-calientes, military convoys travelled overland to La Realidad and beyond. They found the villages deserted. All the people from La Realidad had gone higher up the mountains. 'We were told we were going to leave town and take shelter in the mountains because the soldiers were coming', explains Ruth. The children were crying with hunger and thirst and after sleeping out in the open. Gastrointestinal and respiratory diseases were wreaking havoc with the health of the Tojolabal people. A mother recalls:

- There were a lot of problems in the mountains with mosquitoes and the kids were running high fevers...

The actress Ofelia Medina and two young women from Mexico City who were acting as observers, accompanying the community, offered themselves to guarantee the safety of the indigenous people if they returned home. So return they did.

- We didn't want to carry on hiding anymore, there was too much suffering, the kids crying, going hungry, thirsty... We returned the afternoon they left.

The soldiers had removed all the sharp-pointed stakes which the *campesinos* had placed to deter parachutists or helicopters. That same day 'we replaced them' recalls elderly Teresa.

The following morning eight combat tanks passed near the village and returned at night without stopping. Three days later they returned but in greater number. They came into the village with 'humanitarian aid' and were willing to do 'social labour'.

Ruth explains:

- Here were seventy or eighty soldiers in ten trucks. We could hear their trucks approaching from behind the church. They were waving their guns and shouting through this machine-thing (megaphone) for people to come forward, not to be afraid, because they were not going to harm us, that they came in peace. Peace, ha, no bloody way!

The young city women accompaniers received them. Their attempts to get the soldiers to leave were unsuccessful. Ruth continues:

-The two women went to talk to them and said not to come into the village because the women and children here are afraid of them and don't want them around. But the soldiers replied: 'What do you know, you are not from here. You are foreigners, you don't belong here.'

At that point the villagers decided to take the matter into their own hands.

- We gathered a group of seven women and went to talk to them to say that we don't want them shouting or offering things. And when we went up to them they said:

'Good morning, are you women coming to receive the food that we are bringing?'

'No, we replied, we come to say thank you but no thank you. We are not asking for anything and don't want anything from you; thank you for bothering, but no thank you. We don't want medicine from you because the kids are so frightened of you, in fact the women also, that they fall sick.'

'Why are you afraid of us, ladies? We do you no harm, we are just bringing food, a gift from the government.'

'It can be a gift - it can be bloody anything - we don't want it'

'Ah, this lady doesn't want anything, well she must be a Zapatista's wife!'

'Listen, sir, we know nothing of that, only rumours...'

'Well then, why not receive what we bring, Nueva Providencia and San Quentín are with us'.

'Perhaps, but that's not here. This place is called La Realidad and we don't accept what you bring because we are not the only ones who are needy. If the government feels that the *campesinos* are in need then it should help everyone, not just one or two villages. But in fact the government has no idea what we need. Instead it sends more soldiers, more tanks, more machine-guns. That's the government medicine.'

Another woman added:

'Over there is Nueva Providencia, here is Realidad. This *ejido* is free territory', she said loud and clear.

And the soldiers just stared at me and at each other.

'Well, señora, even though you don't want to hear this, I will speak…'

'No señor, we don't want the army in this village, what we want is for them to withdraw, to go away now, that is what we want.'

'Oh, so these women don't want anything, nothing at all: that's because they are leaders and they don't want anything.'

'That's right, not even medicine because we have been helped already by the people who do care about us, the civil society people who have given us medicine.'

'And who is the promoter?'

'We all are, all of us.'

'Oh well, these women don't want anything.'

Ruth pauses for breath.

- The soldiers got really furious. 'They don't want anything' they were saying. And what a lot of photos they took of us, up close in our faces and of our bodies as well. They said they would beat us and whip us.

'What these women want is a taste of guns; they want a good hiding.'

'Come what may, we are not frightened of death.'

Then elderly Teresa, the village midwife, intervened. Boldly, bravely, she spat at the soldiers.

'We don't need that handful of food you've got there; that's not enough for our village, there's a lot of us. We want tons, for the whole country too, not just in Chiapas. If you want to help, then don't lie. The government is lying to us.'

The soldiers started to talk about the two *ladino* women from the city:

'We can see that these city women are organising you, those

women with glasses on, they are telling you what to do but they are tricking you, don't believe them, don't believe people from outside, they come from another country.'

'They are not organising us and we know who they are. Get out of our village, we are the ones who give the orders here, no one else. There's the road, off you go, if you have to pass close by then keep out of our way, we don't want you bothering us.'

Ruth explains that it was then that the women decided to withdraw and prepare a different strategy.

- We went away and organised all the village women, just the women. 'We have to shout so that they will go away, unless you think you want what they are offering?' No.

'Well, then let's tell them.'

'Let's tell them that we are not prepared to accept what they are offering.'

- We were about a hundred and thirty women, all the women in the community, only about ten didn't come, they were afraid. Some children were with us.

Together they advanced boldly towards the soldiers and their vehicles. When they saw them coming, Ruth and her sister tell us:

- They said 'There come the señoras to get the gifts.' But they became ashamed standing there with the bags they were carrying, for we didn't take them, we told them that no one would come any closer because of their weapons, we were afraid, how did they expect the children to approach them and talk to them?

'No, Señora, we won't hurt you.'

'But we don't want you here.'

'Ah well, we'll come every day until you get used to us, in fact we're going to stay overnight here in La Realidad.'

'We don't want you here, we want you to go away, we are not used to being looked after.'

All the women in the community were there, all the women talking at the same time in their different languages, some in Tojolabal, others in Spanish:

'Bloody government, don't they say they want peace? And here they send their submachine guns and tanks, this is not peace, it's a lie.'

100

'Ah, so you are Zapata's women.'

'We don't know who that is. Is he a person or an animal? No, we don't know him. What we do know is that you have a *zapato* (shoe) which you wear, and which we don't have.

The soldiers were just staring. Then the one with the loudspeaker said:

'No, Señora, listen... I'm going to help you understand...'

'But we don't want to. The government isn't really helping us, it exploits us, taking the things we harvest almost for free. The government is too self-satisfied, sitting in its armchair like a god, worshipping its wealth, because it has no other god.'

'Oh, how these señoras talk... The thing is they are organised, what they need is a few whippings.'

'Well, then we're going to bring a whip too and you'll feel a touch of it too.'

Ruth remembers how they just kept staring at us. Another old lady railed at them:

'Look, I came here with my little bundle of firewood, that's how we eat all the time. In the rainy season, we get soaked carrying our load, we carry our maize, we bend double in the maize field, working with machetes. You try working like us, you couldn't cope because you aren't used to it, you are just used to sitting in your cars. We don't want you here bothering us when we pass by or fetch wood.'

'Ah, but we're going to support you, we will accompany you to cut wood.'

'We don't need the army to come along, we are used to walking alone and we don't want you getting in our way.'

'All right then, tell me, who organised you?'

'Well, nobody did, if an animal thinks, for example how to walk through mud without getting stuck, then can't a person? Just because we can't pronounce the words right you say we don't know anything, that we don't think. Nobody is organising us. We don't need it. One always thinks what one should do.'

'Let's go. OK, Señora, we're leaving, bye.'

The soldiers have left La Realidad alone since then, although almost every day they drive through the village without stopping.

The people s resistance

The indigenous women have waged several battles since it all began, since that first of January when life in Chiapas changed.

Ocosingo, 6th January 1994. There is a long queue of women in front of the smoke-blackened Town Hall. They are waiting for the soldiers to give them a bag with food: sugar, salt, rice, soap, oil, soup, biscuits. However not all of them receive their provisions as they didn't reckon on the soldiers demanding they bring their husbands. If the man isn't there, it's because he is a Zapatista, the soldiers say. Stigmatised, fearful and hungry, the mothers leave. A year later, in February 1995, they no longer go to ask for whatever the government wishes to give, rather they refuse to accept any help.

Patihuitz, 13th February 1995. A convoy of journalists arrive in the valley. The soldiers with their tanks are summoning the civilian population by loudspeaker. They come to offer provisions and to do the 'social work' that has not been done for thirteen months in this Zapatista territory. No one approaches. The TV cameras film the unwanted soldiers. One of them grabs a girl by the arm and forces her to come to the truck and gives her a bag. The young Tzeltal girl gives in, the soldiers smile as, finally, she takes the 'help' but walks twenty metres and throws it in a ditch. She runs away, gaily coloured dress and braids flying in the wind.

February, March, April 1995. The village of Guadalupe Tepeyac is in exodus. Guadalupe Tepeyac, the newest forest village, one hundred per cent Zapatista, one hundred per cent assembly participation, one hundred per cent acceptance of their destiny of resistance.

On 9th February the entire population of Guadalupe Tepeyac has left the village. Even a woman who had just given birth, a sixteen year-old girl who had her first son squatting among the mountain rocks. Several more children came along the way, born during the first days of sleeping crowded together, some premature, because of the mother's fright and weariness. They would be christened at a party in one of the villages that sheltered and fed them for some weeks, a dirt-poor village that nevertheless shared the little they had, in a terrible solidarity of poverty. The Guadalupans, in exchange, left

102

them running water and the pride of greeting adversity with a positive spirit and ability to party, all together, always, with a deep-rooted sense of community.

Guadalupe Tepeyac is treated with wariness because the girls sometimes wear trousers, which is seen as outrageous by other Tojolabal communities. They wore them when carrying *comales* and pans in one of their exodus deeper into the forest, in search of shelter, with the mothers breast-feeding their babies, their few horses and men bowed under their loads, all moving to a safe place, moving in line like ants. The young Guadalupan girls are distinctive in that they are not timid or selfless. They wear simple skirts, white trainers, socks carefully folded over, T-shirts with floral designs, colourful bows and balaclavas with 'EZLN' embroidered on them. On special occasions, the single girls put on some lipstick, eye shadow, blusher and off they go challenging the world. Watching them you think, things have already changed, or as Comandante Trini says: 'the path is already being cleared.'

In July 1996, Guadalupe Tepeyac was still in exile. The villagers built a new Guadalupe. 'Where?' asked a journalist.

'In the heart of the forest', answered Comandante Tacho unhesitatingly. Men cut down trees, opened paths, built new houses for everyone. The women, who had lost everything, had to get used to the newness, to privation, to the bitter memory of their old houses, full of flowers, with patios, kitchens stocked with pots and pans. As Doña Herminia, the oldest of the Guadalupans summed up, it means, 'starting all over, again.' The army's February incursion left its mark of pain and hatred on the rest of the Zapatista area. Men and women from El Prado, in the Tzeltal gully, returned to their village after enduring hunger and cold in the mountains. They couldn't believe their eyes, for the soldiers had shown no mercy at their poverty. Fireplaces were destroyed, mills broken, kitchenware was missing, some houses burned, maize strewn everywhere, the few beans pissed and shat on, clothes torn into shreds. How the people of El Prado grieved that March morning, as they returned to see their homes destroyed. Nothing remained in one piece, not a single machete, not a single axe, not a musical instrument or a book. The solar cell providing power to the village was destroyed, the water pipes shattered into a thousand pieces.

Wailing women raised their arms to heaven and opened their empty hands. *'Pisil'* they said, meaning 'everything' in Tzeltal... absolutely everything destroyed. Then they went into their houses and registered the general destruction. They wanted the video camera to register it all, to record the pain, the extremely high price they had to pay. At the other end of the village a man and a woman carried three children through a heap of ashes. They look bewildered and the children don't dare cry. The ashes are all that is left of their house. 'Here was the bed, here the kitchen', pointed out the man, bowed down. The hours passed. On that same afternoon we left the village to its pain. The family hadn't moved from the ashes. The woman was cradling the children, also unable to cry. A frightful, unforgettable scene. They will spend the night there. There are no walls or roof, but it is still their home. Days later, after an assembly decision and with the help of all the village men, a new hut was built.

In the Altamirano gully, the Morelia *ejido* was considered the 'pearl of the new life'. In 1994 it began an exemplary process of autonomy, recovering ancestral law and appointing its own government authorities: a General Assembly and Senior Citizens' Council. But it had to be hurriedly abandoned, as soldiers were less than half an hour away as they fled barefoot. Wherever the Morelians went people joined them, even whole villages. The women's and children's feet were blistering. For lack of water they drank from any puddle, and gastrointestinal diseases spread like wildfire. Several women became mothers on the way or upon arrival in the mountains.

In Los Altos de Chiapas there was also alarm. Many craftswomen say they worked on their weaving at night because during the day, marked as Zapatistas, they had to leave their homes for the cold Tzotzil mountains.

During May 1995, Bateatón, a few kilometres from Patihuitz, Ocosingo, had to put up with soldiers shooting into the air as part of routine training. 'We want the soldiers out and to stop bothering ordinary people', the villagers told the Human Rights observers.

- Women can't go out for a walk or to the maize field. We are poor and women work all the time, but now they're afraid because they have never seen someone like that, wearing shorts and uniform, soldiers coming daily and messing around.

Get the army out of the forest

On the other edge of the Lacandon forest, in June 1995, during a consultation assembly with the Zapatista grassroots support about the peace negotiations, we listened to the women representatives' fiery speeches. One after the other, the three of them spoke to more than four hundred Tojolabales and fourteen journalists. We had walked non-stop for two days to be there.

'Get the Army out!', shouted the women, fists raised. Gabriela, leaving her breast-feeding baby with her neighbour to stand in front of the assembled circle, read her speech in impeccable Spanish:

- We consider our demands are fair, that's why we thought the government was going to meet them, but unfortunately we can see they don't want peace, because instead of solutions they sent the army to provoke us. This just upsets the poor *campesino compañeros*. Wherever the federal soldiers arrive they prevent us working peacefully, the first thing they do is ask us questions aggressively, threatening us. In the villages, they give orders that have to be fulfilled, threatening us with their weapons, and we are sick of it.

After Gabriela a young girl called Hermelinda stood up. She was also dressed colourfully and sporting the latest fashion in the forest, a belt with a metallic butterfly clasp. Clutching the microphone tightly, her face covered with a brightly coloured scarf she said:

- The soldiers are now all over our land, we can't do our work, when we go to our maize fields they are walking on the road. They scare us, they threaten us and we women can't walk alone if they are around, and sometimes when we go out to look for medicines or to buy provisions, we are afraid. Army: get out!

Irene, the third speaker, came forward, keen to show the national dimension of the problem.

- The situation of women in Mexico is that, besides living in extreme poverty, we are forgotten, even though it is the *campesino* women who work the most for the nation's progress. We work in the fields, we are housewives, we don't have anything to make our work easier. The government has never cared about us, maybe because we can't speak Spanish well, because they say our mother tongue isn't good enough and we can't use any machines or tools. But the contrary is true: we are capable, but what we lack is a little respect for our dignity. We need services here. The smoke from the firewood in the kitchen hurts our eyes...

Discussion of the *campesino* women's domestic working conditions was lengthy. Irene continued:

- No one has ever worried about smoke in our eyes, smoke in our faces, lungs, not just once a day but every single time we have to cook maize, boil water, make the *tortillas*, put the beans to cook, or prepare coffee. Which means all the time. And Mexico is a big world producer of natural gas; at the same time people complain that we have fewer trees every day, but how else can we make our fires?

In the Zapatista community of Agua Azul, two days walking south from La Realidad, we fourteen tired journalists were fed by the organised women of the community: chicken soup, beans, freshly made *tortillas*, eggs. Many of the children there had hardly ever seen visitors before. Their generosity was overwhelming. People's expectancy at our arrival, at the successful outcome of the consultative assembly, our tiredness and the tremendous hospitality, culminated in a quite unprecedented fashion. 'Well, now, the señores journalists are going to talk to us about themselves.' So we began, one by one, to tell the men, women and wide-eyed children about our particular experiences of the war on New Year's Day, and the surprise Zapatista action of 1994. The war, their struggle, was real, it existed beyond them, we were the living proof.

Rape as an instrument of counterinsurgency

In the negotiations on Culture and Indigenous Women's Rights, from the 18-22 October 1995, the women participants and advisers for the government and EZLN reached the following agreement:

- Rape in conflict zones must be considered as a war crime in accordance with international conventions. Further, justice must be done as regards the rape of the Tzeltal women in Altamirano on the 4th of June 1994 and the rape of three nurses in the municipality of San Andrés Larráinzar on the 4th of October 1995.

Soon after, on the 26th of October, the EZLN representative to the United States, Cecilia Rodríguez, when on a tourist visit to the Montebello Lakes, was raped by men wearing balaclavas and armed to the teeth. The attack was similar to that on the three nurses in San Andrés, by supposed Zapatistas who many people believe were soldiers in disguise. Rape, performed by white paramilitaries, hooded men or soldiers, seemed to be increasingly used as a humiliating counterinsurgent weapon. Perhaps because the greatest work for peace in conflict areas was being done by women. Like a dark bird bringing horror and death, impunity reigns still, demonstrating that there is no justice in Mexico, and least of all for women.

On 4th June 1994 three Tzeltal girls were gang-raped at the Altamirano military checkpoint. The three sisters were on their way to sell vegetables at the market. Marta Figueroa, the lawyer who took up the case, explained how hard it was for the women to have the soldiers searching them during those months:

- To them, any physical contact is aggressive, being looked in the eyes is like telling them 'you are hiding your heart from me, I want to see it'. Physical contact is even worse. The soldiers did body searches and which were often obviously lascivious. These Morelian women, had to go through three military checkpoints and admit they tried to avoid them. Their father wasn't with them, he had left to live with another woman. They've struggled alone since they were little. The land they worked on was never going to be theirs because it was registered under their father's name and as there wasn't a son it passed to their uncle, who kept them working the land.

After they were raped they agreed to denounce the events to Conpaz, the Non Governmental Organisations' Human Rights Co-ordination Committee. Their statement was immediately published in the papers.

- The Mexican army started looking for them, they knew which community they were from because they took their personal details every time they passed an army checkpoint. That information went to the National Commission on Human Rights (a government institution) which tried to put pressure on them to change their testimony. That's why we are charging them as well - says Marta Figueroa - and for a long time they tried to negotiate a withdrawal of the charge. Then the soldiers went to their community and harassed everyone.

To these women the nightmare wasn't over with their formal complaint, quite the opposite:

- They are frightened because they were told that if they denounced the rape, they would be killed. So then they have two reasons to run away, to protect themselves and because the whole community, even though they are relatives, begins to put pressure on them to leave because they are afraid the soldiers will continue to harass them if they are still there. They went to another community, a Zapatista one, as they had no choice in the matter. They know the Mexican army can't go there, so they feel more or less safe. The community puts a little pressure on them to continue with the complaint, perhaps in exchange for the accommodation.

- They were used politically, by the community, by Conpaz, which gave their statement to the press. I almost had a heart attack because I was so angry. In rape cases, a basic rule of the Group is secrecy, you do not give information away, particularly to the press, we can't make public the names of either the victims or perpetrators. The next day a government bulletin stated these women didn't exist, that they were the product of the journalists' imagination and that they reserve the right to sue us for libel against the Mexican army. The only way to put a stop to that was for them to confirm the facts. But they were in a bad state, they hardly speak Spanish and we couldn't provide them with emotional support via therapy.

Figueroa explains she was reconciling herself to the idea of losing the case when 'after a month and because of the community's pressure, two of them, Teresa and Cristina, confirmed the whole thing to the Federal Attorney's Office which then provided legal protection.'

- The Attorney's Offices attitude was 'I don't believe a thing, who is going to bother raping these filthy Indians?' But then he listened to their story, via translation, and saw how Teresa, the eldest one, drew a map of the place where she was raped, and although she holds the pencil like this, with her fist, her strokes are firm and confident and strong. The drawings and timing indicate that the eldest knows more. She is an exceptional woman, extremely intelligent, very affected, but stronger than her sisters. She says she is twenty years-old but if you see her you wouldn't think she's older than sixteen.

The Attorney General's Office apologised to the lawyer for doubting the authenticity of the complaint, but since then the Ministry of Defence insists it is their jurisdiction, it remains unsolved. Figueroa protested:

- We said that when civilians are implicated there has to be civil trial. That's why we made two appeals, to the Federal Ombudsman and to the Ministry of Defence, but both were rejected. So the soldiers start summoning me, the second notification was delivered by armed men driving a jeep. It said that if I didn't show up, force would be used on me, and that I had to bring the girls. So I went and told them that I didn't acknowledge their authority and that they could go to hell.

A few days afterwards, Marta Figueroa was summoned again to a line-up of soldiers on duty the day of the rape:

- I heard how they were questioned, how they contradicted each other, I noticed they were so nervous it was obvious they'd participated, at least two of them.

The lawyer refused to bring the girls and could therefore be accused of obstructing justice:

- I didn't want to make them pass two army checkpoints, bring them to the military base, to a military doctor to be examined and then interrogated and treated as libel suspects. 'You are crazy, I will never bring them to you', I said. All these procedures and appeals took a long time.

In February 1995, when the federal army entered Zapatista territory, the three sisters, along with the rest of the people in Altamirano gully, began an exodus deep into the forest. Marta lost track of them:

- We didn't find them until May, we explained the situation again but they didn't want to know, they have started their life again somewhere else, with another name, other circumstances. The only option we have now is to make an international denunciation with all the evidence, whether the girls are present or not. If it proceeds and their physical presence is required, I expect after so much time they will be a little more relaxed. But they see us bringing this case as a threat to their new stability.

Chapter 6

Everyday life in Los Altos de Chiapas

Far from the steamy forest, Los Altos de Chiapas mountain range seems to be perpetually veiled in a mysterious white mist. At midday the mountains shine brilliantly green against the intense blue sky. At night they form deep dark caverns. It is the land of the Tzotzil, who call themselves 'bat men and women', men and women of the night.

The indigenous women there wear blue or yellow or Zinacanteca pink shawls. They get up at dawn. First they light the fire and then they begin to heat water for their husbands and children to wash their faces and hands; they will keep it hot through the day for many other chores. Then the woman cleans the house and washes and grinds the maize to make the *tortillas*. When she finishes with the *tortillas*, she has breakfast with her husband and her children, who are just coming back from fetching firewood: this is when they tell each other what they've dreamt or what is going on in the community with relatives, friends, or what religious or civil tasks they might have. They share their ideas and organise the day. Then she does the washing up and puts the food under cover. Then she cleans the patio and sometimes goes to deliver some *pozol* to her husband's workplace. Once back she goes to the stream to do the washing, look after the smaller children and the sheep or to bring more firewood. When the *pozol* runs out, she boils some more, until the maize has risen and then she starts grinding again. Right away she starts cooking so the meal will be ready when her husband and the children are back from work or school. Then she boils the maize for the next day. After dinner, exhausted by her labours she falls asleep.

(From a paper by María Santiz and María Hernández, both from Chamula; Rosenda de la Cruz and Margarita López, from Zinacantán, and Lucía Santiz, from Tenejapa, all members of the indigenous cultural organisation, Sna Jtz'ibajom.)

The guardian spirits, our father-mothers

The Tzotzil women say that:

When K'ox, the Sun God, was little, his mother Moon protected him from the evildoers who wanted to hurt him. Our mother Moon gave advice to women on how to look after their children, how to weave, what to do to improve their lives, how to pray and serve their people in civil and religious duties.

(Sna Jtz'ibajom).

The teachings of the moon have lasted until today. The night star, say the indigenous women, stills sends her messages to her sons and daughters through dreams.

- That's why a good mother always asks her children what they dreamt, so that she knows how to pray and look after their souls, the most important thing in our lives - explains María Santiz.

- Our mothers start to give us advice when we are young girls: 'when you have a child don't feed him from a bottle, the breast is better so that he will grow up healthy; you have to eat well too... When he learns how to feed himself, don't let anyone give him coffee or soft drinks...

The mother will bring up her child in a different way if it is a girl or a boy. A group of Tzotzil girls summed up:

- Children first learn our mother tongue. The mother basically is in charge of teaching the child. Then the father teaches him more things, by example: how to chop firewood, make fences, work the land and sow maize, beans and other crops, and to look after domestic animals. From his grandparents and parents religious beliefs are learnt and how to behave when meeting with people in parties and the carnival. These days many boys finish primary school and in some communities even secondary school. Some of them can get jobs as drivers, mechanics, traders, builders, domestic workers.

112

The few who are bilingual and literate in both languages can get jobs as promoters or technicians. Others go as temporary farm workers to Tabasco or even to the United States. Many of them are already forgetting our culture. Some leave and never come back. But most of them come back to speak their mother tongue again, to be with their family celebrating the Patron Saints' holidays and the carnival, to feel the satisfaction of being in their homeland.

Their future is marked by being born into poverty. There is no way women can aspire to a profession, they are condemned to exploitation and housework from an early age.

- Girls are brought up to get up early, to clean the house, make *tortillas*, do the washing up, the washing, prepare the meals, weave, embroider, fetch wood. Some also learn to tend sheep, duties like that. Wearing traditional costume is still the practice... Other mothers don't know how to bring their daughters up properly, they want to do it by telling them off: if they don't learn quickly how to make *tortillas*, they put their hands on the hot *comal* or smoke their faces with the smoke coming out of the chillies in the fireplace until they cry. But that isn't good education; children can get ill in the future, especially if they are struck in the head.

Maruch, the Chamula photographer

Maruch means María in Tzotzil. The press photographers at San Cristóbal mentioned her. Who is Maruch? She is a Chamula photographer who takes extraordinary black and white photos. You are going to write about women? And you haven't interviewed Maruch yet? In October 1995, I went to the office of Sna Jtz'ibajom in San Cristóbal, where Maruch works, although every day she treks back to her community and to her parents.

- My name is María Santiz Gómez, native of Crustón, municipality of Chamula. I am twenty years old. I started on this job because I had a cousin who asked me if I would like to come and take a drama course and learn to write in Tzotzil and I told him yes. In October 1995, the photographic laboratory was built and they taught us.

Maruch wears her traditional Chamula costume, blue shawl,

113

thick black skirt of virgin wool, blue blouse, plastic sandals. Several magazines have published her photos which aim to recreate the Tzotzil cultural universe. She explains:

- There aren't any indigenous people taking photos. The journalists come but it isn't the same, they don't know how to give the right meaning to the images, or about the parties and the costumes.

- I think I'm the only indigenous photographer, because to be honest I haven't heard of a Tzotzil, Tzeltal, Tojolabal photographer... even though it would be nice if there was. I like photography because people who can't read and write can see photos and that way our traditions don't get lost.

To discover the meaning of some of the images she had to ask the old people.

- It is hard because my parents no longer know the old meanings of things and I have to go to other communities to do research. The old people ask me,

'What is this for? How much is it worth?'

And I tell them that I just want to know what it means because it is nearly all being forgotten.

'Yes well, you are right about that... but tell us where you are from or we will call the village policeman.'

'But why? I was born here.'

'Oh that's all right then.'

That's the way my work goes.

-The idea of preserving traditions through photographs was my own idea. Given that I had already written down the beliefs, I wanted to find the right photos to accompany the text.

Maruch's life has been the same as that of many indigenous women.

- My father left when I was little, I don't know why, we were poor, so he went to look for work when my mother was two months pregnant with me. By the time he returned I was walking. He was away almost three years. My mother had to look for a godmother for me, it was my grandmother, there was no one else to christen me. When my father returned, my mother said to me: 'this is your father

114

who was not here when you were born.' I was afraid of my father because I didn't know him.

Tzotzil shepherds

The women in Los Altos start work as shepherdesses from a tender age. They work outside in the fields and woods. Seated on rocks they embroider or walk solitary paths accompanied only by their flock. These women form a special relationship with the animals with which they spend such long hours. The sheep only serve to provide wool for weaving the traditional garments. They die of old age or disease but are not eaten. The women speak to them and care for them. It is not unusual to see the sheep carefully adorned with pieces of coloured plastic sheeting to protect them from the rain whilst their owners get soaked, 'otherwise the sheep get a cold.'

Maruch spent a lot of her life as a shepherdess.

- Every sheep has a name, something to do with its colour perhaps. Or people's names, we call them Andrea or Dominga if they are female. If the sheep has brown or black patches then it's called 'piebald' or if it is brown all over, then 'Chacshic' which means coffee in Tzotzil, or if it's snow-white then 'Shingan' the name of a sacred virgin who was very pretty.

Maruch explains the complicated psychology of these particularly sensitive animals:

- I like to be with the sheep because if you like looking after them, then they behave well and get nice and fat and give lots of good wool. But there are people who don't like sheep and don't care for them properly. Then they die, they get thin and poorly, they get spots and fleas, different types of fleas which grow in the fleece around their neck and then spread all over 'til you can hardly see anything but fleas. If they are well cared for, rotating a while on the mountain, a while in the paddock, then they feel good and won't stray. But there are sheep which escape. And we can get angry with them if they won't eat or don't let us sit down. I think it depends on the way their owners treat them.

Lorena Gómez González is twenty-three. She is a Tzotzil from

115

Chenalhó and a past chairwoman of the J'pas Joloviletik Weavers' Co-operative. Her life has much in common with that of Maruch.

- I am the eldest of six; three girls, three boys. When we were young, we girls had to go off each day with the flock and if our little brothers wanted to, they could come too. It was hard when it rained. We would just stop wherever we were because we were not supposed to return until five in the afternoon when the sheep had grazed sufficiently. I like tending the sheep but where we are now there is no grazing nearby and we have to walk for an hour or two to find good pastures.

Lorena explains:

- Men don't work as shepherds, only the women. The men just work in the maize field, and tend to the harvest. They don't learn to weave either. Girls work more than boys because they have to cook, weave, and also work in the fields and look after the sheep.

Maruch, like many other Chamulas, has an anecdote about sheep which she loves to tell:

- When I was four years old my mother sent me off to look after the sheep. It was a large flock of about twenty-five. My mother would go to dig new ground and carry wood with my older sister who was six by then. Once one of the sheep pushed me into the river and I nearly drowned. It butted me with its horn and I was only four years old and all alone! It still makes me frightened when I remember it. That was the only sheep that gave me problems, it was called 'big horn' , the only one with horns. When I got home my mother asked me: 'what happened to you, why are you wet?'

And I told her what happened, but she still sent me to shepherd them. She said:

'I think you were playing with the lamb and that's why he pushed you.'

On another occasion we were feeding the flock from some trees on the mountain and the same lamb butted me again, nearly over the edge. This time my mother believed me.

'It must be true that you weren't playing' and she killed it, I still remember; it was called 'big horn Lechjol'. Sometimes I remind my mum and we laugh about it again.

116

Maruch remained in charge of the flock.

- When I was five they sent me to school. After school finished I would take two or three *tortillas* with salt and go look after the sheep which my mother had been tending during the day. That left her free to go home and prepare the *nixtamales*. She did everything, made our clothes and tended the maize fields. The Chamula women don't actually sow the seed, they just prepare the ground and the people from other villages sow. I liked learning, so did my sister, but as there was no one to tend the sheep my mother went to the school to withdraw my sister and only I stayed in school.

When Maruch finished fifth grade primary her mother said:

- 'You had better leave now, because there's too much work. It would be better that you work here at home.'

I felt very sad because it was like I had wasted five years in primary school for nothing. So I said to my father: 'I want to go on studying.'

'So, where will you go?'

'Well I thought I would go to Romerillo.'

'Well you can't go until next year, because no pupils will be accepted now.'

'So while I was waiting I started to make skirts, petticoats, jackets, overcoats from our wool. I carded the wool and wove it, everything. The next year I went to Romerillo. Every day, a forty-minute walk to get there and all I had to eat was the same as when I was little, *tortilla* with salt and cabbage and sometimes a few beans; other people eat quite a lot of beans but we didn't have the money to buy them.

An absurd education system

Maruch is eager to talk about the absurd and difficult education in indigenous communities:

- The truth is that in primary school I didn't understand Spanish at all. I didn't understand anything. Because the teachers come and read to us, they finish reading and say 'copy this drawing'. And I didn't know what the letters meant. They don't teach us well and that's why it was useless. When I finished I didn't understand anything. Even though the teachers are bilingual, they are ashamed. I've seen many, many people who were ashamed about not knowing Spanish.

- Then I went to secondary school, where they teach only in Spanish. Teachers in primary school talk only in Tzotzil and they say 'read' and 'copy' and that's it. As regards reading, yes we know how to read and write, but we don't know what it means, that's the problem. In secondary school they ask us what we understand of a text, and we have to say, 'well it was too difficult, I didn't understand.'

Then the teachers ask: 'Why don't you know any Spanish? Why don't you understand?'

'Because the primary teachers didn't teach us.'

According to article three of the Constitution of the Mexican Republic, primary education is compulsory for all children. In Los Altos de Chiapas and the Lacandon forest this obligation is not respected, especially for the girls. France J. Falquet, in his anthropological study *Las mujeres indigenas de Chiapas de cara a la escuela* (Inaremac, 1995), highlights three main features of state education: low attendance, high drop-out rate between first and sixth grades and always fewer girls than boys in the classroom.

In December 1994, when the new Zapatista municipalities were launched, one of the first measures taken by the *campesinos* was to deny access to the teachers until a general education plan was defined and approved by the communities in accordance with indigenous culture and needs. This was basically because education as it stands is seen to function as a 'brainwashing into a foreign culture'.

The point has been made that the practice of excluding girls from the education system serves communities as a device for cultural resistance. Women, little in contact with the external world, are the guardians of custom, tradition and language. However, the price they pay is ignorance, social immobility and subjugation.

In Tzotzil communities, there are few girls whose parents don't object to them studying or going out. Maruch says she was lucky:

- My father always let me, always. But usually girls are not sent to school, their parents don't allow them. My father is the only one in

118

the family; my uncles don't give my cousins permission. They say, 'It's expensive and what's the point?'. All my cousins, boys and girls, work in the fields. But after I finished school and I went back to being a shepherdess again I didn't like it very much.

Fortunately Maruch managed to pass an entrance exam to study in Sna Jtz'ibajom. There she learnt to write in Tzotzil, and worked on recovering some of the old myths and legends.

- I wrote a story called Two Shepherds. When I finished I started another which I'm just finishing called: The Man and His Nagual. It's about some people who live in the mountains with lots of animals (sheep, chickens, turkeys), and a man wanted them to sell one but they wouldn't. But he had a strong *nagual*, a coyote. Anyway it's quite long, nine pages.

There are no female characters in Maruch's stories. Perhaps in this respect her imagination is limited by living in a sexist society. She has to struggle to achieve what she wants.

- My parents are happy. Although some people are jealous and spread lies about me having a boyfriend. They also say I'm a streetwalker, not an office-worker. But my mother doesn't believe them. When he is in his right mind my father doesn't either but when he's drunk he believes them and gets angry and shouts at me. A while back my uncle said to him 'your daughter is out with some people, she has a lot of friends.' My father answered: 'well you may be right but why are you telling me?'

'Because she is talking with men, with the son of so-and-so.'

My father knows the fathers of the boys mentioned so he scolds my mother:

' I've been told that our daughter has been talking with the son of so-and-so.'

'But why do you think that; these men are married'.

'Because my brother told me so.'

'Well I'm sorry he's telling lies.'

So then my father said to me:

'It would be better if you left my house, I no longer want to see your face here.'

I just waited until he was in his right mind again and then I said:

'All right then father, I shall leave but give me the money I gave you to repair the house because I need it if I am going.'

Then my father cried, really cried, 'I'm sorry, but it's what your uncle said.'

'He can say what he likes, but the fact is that he is angry because he wanted us to lend him money and we didn't, so now he is spreading lies,' I replied.

Maruch is not interested in village gossip.

- There are people who think that what I am doing is not proper work. They think I am crazy. Some think that we must keep our customs, as things were done in the past and that women should not go out. But the rest of them are just plain jealous. Actually there has never been an actress or a bilingual writer in our community; there aren't any. There are some teachers but they can't write in their mother tongue. I have friends in the community who are ashamed to speak in their mother tongue. I said to them:

'How can you forget our mother tongue? As a teacher you should use it.'

Maruch really loves her culture and, to the surprise of those of us who have only seen poverty and exploitation in the lives of indigenous women, she speaks of beauty.

- The traditional work we do is wonderful. I think it is wonderful that the women still embroider and weave and that we have not lost our culture and our crafts; I love the work we do.

When asked about the Zapatistas, Maruch is cautious.

- Well I think that the uprising was good because when indigenous people ask the government for things they always refuse; they say yes, but nothing ever happens. I think that's why the Zapatistas got together. I was surprised to see women with guns, yes, for example Ramona.

The EZLN and how the women woke up

Lorenza has a big smile. We asked her the same question we asked Maruch about whether her father let her go to secondary school.

'Well, before, no' and she laughs. The 'before' refers to before the EZLN had any influence.

- I wanted to go on studying but my father wouldn't let me, because he said I was only looking for a boyfriend. In fact that is the case sometimes. So I didn't go. But neither did my brothers. My youngest brother was the only one given permission, but of course he was the only one who did not want to go.

Like Maruch, Lorenza had to go back to tend the flock.

- When I finished primary school I returned to my community and had to go back to looking after the sheep and so on. Back to harvesting the maize, weaving, embroidering, following the flock, fetching wood, fetching water.

However, since the arrival of the EZLN in Los Altos and the passing of the revolutionary laws for women, everything has changed, including Lorenza's father.

- Just recently, I said to my father that I wanted to study. This time he replied: 'do what you want, think about it and make your own decision.' Before I wasn't allowed to do anything, but organisation has changed things and we can now. Before… only the men could take part. But things have changed quite a lot since the Zapatista uprising. And yet, the women who are not organised are just as badly-off as ever, crushed, there's no change there. They don't know what their rights are or what the Zapatistas are doing.

Both Lorenza and her mother have experienced change in their lives.

- My mother thinks it is good because she can go out now. Before, some men wouldn't let their wives out and when they came here to San Cristóbal to sell their cloth the men got very jealous. But things are different now. When there is a meeting in the shop my mother can go. And those who aren't organised are seeing how to do it. Now there are lots of women getting organised.

The weavers: traditional craftswomen

Lorenza says:

- My mother taught me to weave skirts and blouses when I was young, just twelve or thirteen. By the time the daughter is seven the mother has to teach her everything necessary to feed a family. So, she taught me how to grind maize, make *tortilla*, carry water, because we have to carry water, we don't have drinking water and we don't have electricity and we don't have a road...

Besides tending sheep, women in Los Altos de Chiapas learn to weave. Even when western clothes are cheaper these days, Tzotzil women still do their embroidering and traditional clothes. These are part of their cultural legacy and also allow them access to the tourist crafts market.

- We use the waist loom, made from wooden lathes, rope, a leather belt, thread, thin twine and when we're about to finish we use a wooden comb and special wire.

The traditional technique is complex and laborious.

- If the wool is too long, it is cut and then washed with amole, because if you do it with soap the thread won't be good. Then you hang it and when it's dry you separate it into pieces, card it, count it in pairs, thread it and dye it with plants and black soil. Then you get the loom ready, weave, wash the finished product to shrink it and when it's ready you can wear it. For some kinds of textiles, like the *chujes* men wear and the skirts, we use twenty lathes. In the simple ones we use eight. In Tenejapa, people buy *chamarros,* the dyed wool made by the Chamulas. The embroidery in the shorts and belts is made with commercial wool. Some women have learned to card, make thread and dye it with plants for the ceremonial *huipiles,* used specially for virgins, saints and religious duties. In Zinacantán they also use wool and cotton in combination with commercial wool and they don't work with twenty lathes any longer. For the *jerkail* (a kind of pink jacket embroidered with flowers and swinging pompoms) worn by men, twelve lathes are used. For the shawl and the petticoat eight are used and for other garments, nine...

The complicated patterns each village uses in their embroidering are not random. Each figure has a meaning which in many cases the women don't understand, even though they reproduce it. The red rhombus dotted with four different colours represents the four cardinal points. Then there are frogs, men, deer, maize cobs. The indigenous girls in Sna Jtz'ibajom explain:

- In villages such as San Andrés or Magdalena some women still know how the embroidery designs should be woven and what they mean. The ceremonial textiles represent the sacred space where saints and ancient gods live. The number of threads and the arrangement of the designs are prayers used to worship sacred beings. The women who know how to do them are highly respected. In Tenejapa and Chamula, there are women who have special religious duties, such as Me' Sacramento, for which she doesn't need to be married. In other municipalities only men are allowed to worship sacred images.

The J pas Joloviletik co-operative

Lorenza and her mother are weavers, like many women in their village. When she was little, she tells us, they lived through hard times.

- It was difficult for my family, because they didn't know where to sell their clothes. They didn't have money to buy medicines and we often fell ill. There wasn't a doctor, so we had to travel to Chenalhó. Sometimes people died on the way if they didn't get to the doctor quick enough. We had to walk for two hours uphill to get to the town centre.

In August 1995 Lorenza had been president of J'pas Joloviletik for eighteen months.

- I was elected by the women in the assembly, I do enjoy it but sometimes I find it difficult to speak Spanish. Before, I lived in my house, in my community, Culchick, in Chenalhó. I worked in the communities, there we made our clothes, textiles and embroidery.

However, the indigenous women didn't have a place to sell their crafts. So, slowly but surely, supported at first by the National Indigenous Institute and later on their own, the weavers began to get organised. It was in the late seventies when tourists interested in the clothes woven and embroidered by the Tzotzil women started arriving in Los Altos de Chiapas. As a result the indigenous women found a source of extra family income which at the same time encouraged their participation in public life. With the creation of co-operatives, fundamental in regulating their craft, the Tzotzil women set out upon the road to emancipation which the men, impoverished and unemployed, had no option but to acknowledge. It is said that two women from San Andrés Sacamchén, Juana and Pascuala, were the first to realise the need for organisation, at some point during the eighties. At that time there wasn't even an asphalt road. The two of them walked for nine hours to San Cristóbal with their blouses and embroideries.

The women publicised what they were doing and as a result the number of weavers working in co-ordination grew. The National Indigenous Institute gave them legal advice and the Public Education Secretariat gave them premises. Every six years, these institutions made a plan for the Indians but it wasn't one that spoke to their aspirations, they were just welfare measures. During Carlos Salinas de Gortari's administration, the 'Women in Solidarity' initiative was launched. According to Yolanda, a *ladino* adviser for J'pas Joloviletik, this programme failed,

- because once again the same mistake was made, because it wasn't the women who proposed the projects, they were designed to meet the needs of *mestizo* women.

For example, *nixtamal* mills were given to the communities with the idea of reducing women's workload, but without any instructions for use. In some places they couldn't use them because electricity was needed. In other communities they did better by giving petrol-operated mills. However, without operating instructions, many accidents happened and several women almost died in a fire. Thirty-year-old Yolanda, who's been working in Chiapas for ten years, says:

- In my view they only caused problems. Besides, most of those mills were controlled by the local bosses (*caciques*), by men. The SOCAMA (the official trade union) leaders controlled all the mills.

The birth of a project

In the eighties, the National Indigenous Institute (INI), as part of an official policy of respect for cultures and support for traditions, promoted the creation of co-operatives or 'social solidarity societies' which took off to some extent. When the governor visited Los Altos de Chiapas, the Tzotzil craftswomen were called to escort him in their best traditional costume. Lorenza remembers that,

- When the co-operative shop was organised, I was young, but my mother always came here. She suffered a lot because, before, the people who worked here mistreated the women, paid them badly. They had resources for a women's project, but we don't know what they did with the money. So we all got together to get those workers sacked.

In 1992, J'pas Joloviletik changed the way it worked. The structure was democratised and from then on it was the indigenous women representatives in each municipality who established relations with the traders and set prices and conditions. The indigenous women, mostly monolingual and illiterate, were gradually taking over their own space, their resources and their co-operative. Yolanda tells us:

- And then we started lobbying. If the INI wanted to help, then they should support the projects presented by the women, with the proviso that the women manage them and that they should know how much money there was and what it was being spent on. In 1991, I began to work with the co-operative. INI Director Marco Antonio sent buses to the municipalities so the women had free transport to their assemblies. About five hundred of the eight-hundred and seventy-three went, so with transport everyone would come. They also made big pots of food and all of them had beans, rice, *tortilla* and water. So every woman was happy. Those were incredible assemblies.

However when Patrocinio González Garrido became governor of Chiapas (1989-1994), the INI director was accused of mis-appropriation of funds and was sacked. The funding for women's co-operatives was cut off. Yolanda was pressured to leave her post, with the shop windows being broken regularly. And there were more problems.

125

- In one of the assemblies a man showed up posing as a journalist:

'I come to talk to you because many indigenous women and men are going to open a law suit against you for fraud'.

'What fraud?' I asked, 'I don't handle any money!' I had only been in the co-operative for three months.

He said: 'That's what is going to be published, it's going to be a big scandal, in all the papers. But I will make a deal with you.'

So we agreed to discuss it in the shop. I went into the assembly and told everyone about it. All the women were furious, they said:

'Really? Well if he's meeting you, then let's form a committee of some women and men with our own plan. We'll hide in the backroom of the shop and listen to what he says. If it can be recorded, so much the better, so that the women in the other communities can listen to it.'

So the 'journalist' arrived at the office, and I let him explain and when he was about to finish, everyone comes out, they close the shop and surround him. The Spanish-speaking ones stand in front of him and tell him:

'You are not a journalist, you are from the government and want to shit on us. And if you're trying to get money from this *compañera* it's like trying to get money from our organisation.'

So they started insulting him and telling him that they would undress him, cut his hair and make him walk naked around San Cristóbal 'so everyone will know what you are doing to us, because you are insulting us'. The women said:

'Once again you want to shit on us, people like you; you should be ashamed because you even look indigenous and obviously you don't want to acknowledge who you are anymore. You're heartless, you don't want to help your brothers and sisters.'

Yolanda left the shop for the nearest telephone and called El Tiempo. She didn't know the editor, Concepción Villafuerte, but she quickly told her what was happening and Concepción answered

- 'Really? I'll be there right away with two police officers to get that criminal, I'm on my way.'

In a few minutes Doña Concha arrived with the two police, sirens blaring.

'Let's see, you good-for-nothing, show me your identification. Gentlemen, this man is committing extortion.'

Doña Concha made the police arrest him and take him to jail. Then she stayed for a while with the weavers:

'Well, this won't end here. If you want to leave it like that, it'll stay like that, he'll be locked up for a few hours and that's it. If you want to go ahead with this, you'll have to commit yourselves to making a complaint, you will have to go to the Public Ministry and follow it through.'

So everyone answered:

'Let's do it'. So there we all were, in the middle of a downpour, we didn't have a bus at that time but about forty women followed Doña Concha to the Public Ministry. And the women were there, protesting, until one in the morning. It was decided who the witnesses would be, who would speak and what they would say. And we managed to get that man jailed for six months. However, what they wanted most wasn't for him to be punished, but for him to say who sent him. We never found that out.

Yolanda says about Doña Concha:

- She's always worked on her own, she is always on the move. She's a living legend around here.

We are, we exist

J'pas Joloviletik continued their work. It consists of over eight hundred women from twenty-three different communities in Los Altos de Chiapas. In early 1996, because of official pressure against the Zapatista women, many left, including Yolanda. The co-operative made many things change for Tzotzil families. Lucas, the husband of Pascuala, one of the best weavers in Los Altos, is delighted with his wife's participation in J'pas Joloviletik. He says:

- Women have rights, we are all equal. Still, there has to be better organisation so that the rights of women, men and children are known. It is not the same as it was before when the men gave the women orders at home. It's changing slowly but surely.

Yolanda explains that there are some men interested in

participating in the co-operative,

- and you can't tell them they can't because their participation is valuable too, besides they make the project seem important to other men. Also they speak Spanish better and help us translate ideas and concepts from Tzotzil.

A woman weaves provides an essential contribution to the family economy and slowly increases her self-esteem. Indigenous women, abused and undervalued, are used to self-sacrifice. Their inferiority complex is hard to overcome, it is exacerbated by their extreme shyness, fear of the outside world, and depression. The weaver, however, acknowledges herself as indispensable for her family, and acquires self-assurance through her craft.

Marcela, president of J'pas Joloviletik during 1993, suffered physical abuse from her husband. Since joining the co-operative she started gaining strength. She went to other communities and told women: 'My husband beats me and I'm pissed off; I won't take any more.' Everything she had hidden for so many years was beginning to come to the surface. But her husband made more serious threats. He said 'If you go to another meeting I will kill you.'

So she left the presidency and did not attend any other meeting.

Cristina is a *mestiza*, twenty-seven years old, and joined J'pas Joloviletik during 1994-5. Her main job was to run workshops on production costs for the indigenous women.

- We took the garments they make in each municipality to see how many balls of thread they use, how much each ball costs, how many hours a day you sit and weave, how many days it takes you to finish your work and from that work out the real worth of their labour. We agreed we were going to charge fifteen pesos per eight-hour day, which is low but it's what a man earns, so that's why they thought it fair. Then we realised that, for example, the *huipiles* from Larráinzar, which last year were sold in the shops for three hundred pesos, actually cost six hundred in raw materials and working hours, and that doesn't include the preparation of the loom which is difficult, boring and time-consuming. But we also see at what price they can be sold. This type of *huipil* won't be sold for six hundred pesos even though it's worth it.

128

Often a woman who's in real need of money will sell her work for less than cost-price in Santo Domingo market. To Cristina that is a big problem because many weavers don't have the discipline to analyse how much they've paid for the thread. However, this workshop had significant consequences. Cristina tells us about the transformation of the weavers:

- It is incredible how they grow in strength, acquiring their own ideas, becoming more sure of themselves. For example, a *compañera* had been beaten by her husband for many years, but when they both started participating and supporting the organisation the beatings stopped. She became stronger, it's like saying, the income I bring into my family is necessary, it is the difference between being hungry or not.

The Zapatista uprising

When the war broke out on 1st January 1994 the weaver's co-operative resumed energetic activity. It was one of the first organisations to be on the streets, demanding peace and a negotiated solution. As a result of the Zapatista uprising and the Revolutionary Law on Women, discussion and debate and workshops were held on the importance of keeping the customs and traditions of the Indian people but discarding the unjust ones. It was a very sudden awakening, an imperative need to know. Indigenous women began to ask many things, such as 'what does 'human rights' mean?', for the expression doesn't exist in Tzotzil. The weavers' world was being shaken, they were thrust towards learning, participating, taking sides.

From January 1994, says Cristina:

- Women were already talking about politics, they already knew there's a Zapatista movement, they can honestly say whether they agree or not, they can talk about all those centuries of oppression. To me this is key, because it involves their daughters, who are listening to different words and thoughts. The changes will be in the little girls, the young ones, because they are attending the meetings and learning to distinguish between good and bad customs.

All the women of the co-operative were beaming with pride when they saw Comandante Ramona was an EZLN delegate in the first government dialogue in San Cristóbal. Not only because she's a woman, but also Tzotzil and wearing an embroidered *huipil* like those they weave. The J'pas Joloviletik women concluded:

- Ramona tells us we are capable, that we Tzotzil women are powerful, she's telling us we can cope alone.

Yolanda explains that with the appearance of the EZLN armed women, indigenous women became fashionable within the feminist movement:

- Before they didn't even exist. We had the idea of going to the Seventh Feminist Meeting in Acapulco, in the state of Guerrero. Some women from the co-operative went. We took some of our crafts and a short written presentation. However, none of the near one thousand women at that meeting showed interest in the indigenous women. We had to lobby for a statement on the 500 years. I tell them now: 'keep an eye open, for just like the indigenous women there is the urban popular movement, housewives, prostitutes, children... Let's include these sectors in our analysis and give them the chance to participate'. Rosario Robles said that their presence was a demonstration of their existence. But I think they had to take up arms as the only way to make people notice.

Threats and aggression against the co-operative

Open aggression against the co-operative began in May 1994. The weavers had participated not only in each and every peace demonstration but also in the civil security human chain around the Cathedral during the first dialogue between the government and the rebels.

From then on the co-operative premises were watched and besieged. Some nights people entered and searched and were openly threatening. In the mornings the sacks of yarn were scattered or the women found things missing. Two weavers received unexplained visits at home, aimed at extracting information. Around the time that J'pas Joloviletik attended the first meetings of the Chiapan Peoples State Assembly, two soldiers presenting official badges

130

showed up at the shop requesting to talk to Yolanda 'about the conflict in Chiapas'.

On 19 May 1994 a forum for women on the fourth article of the constitution was held. It was eight at night when Yolanda went to her car to go home. When she reached her car, she noticed that behind it there was a Ford van with several men, following her.

- I saw the one near the window bend and reach for something, and they began to load their pistols. I started to run in the opposite direction and they reversed to follow me.

After this, the anonymous phone-calls to the co-operative began. Picking up the telephone Lorenza heard: 'Bloody Indian, we'll kill you.' When Yolanda answered, a male voice told her: 'if you don't stop working we'll kill one of your little Indian girls.'

These threats sowed much fear and anguish among the co-operative women. Some stopped going. One afternoon, Lorenza was alone in the shop. A man entered and tried to hit her. Yolanda was approaching a nervous breakdown and didn't know what to do. Lorenza couldn't take it anymore, she felt she was going to be killed any minute. At J'pas Joloviletik meetings the women sat and cried.

Concepción Villafuerte intervened again. Moving heaven and earth she submitted a denunciation to the National Commission for Human Rights, she spoke to the Department of Defence and made sure that the tale of harassment was published in the *Jornada*.

And the weavers refused to be cowed. Despite this atmosphere of tension and fear, they decided to support Amado Avendaño's campaign as civil society candidate for the government of Chiapas and registered with the Democratic Revolution Party (PRD).

After suffering an 'accident' that almost ended his life, and did end the life of his three companions, Avendaño withdrew, and his wife Conchita took over the campaign. The Tzotzil women felt their strength renewed and continued ahead, realising other organisations were facing the same harassment.

The resistance of the Zapatistas

Lorenza, president of the co-operative, says they are all going through a very difficult stage after the Zapatista uprising.

- We don't sell anymore because there are no tourists; we do our embroideries, our textiles; but we don't know where to sell them, because weeks go by and no clients. I handle the co-operative money so the weavers ask me for money, but how am I going to pay them without sales? In many communities women have to buy maize to eat because they don't have land and sometimes they don't eat because they don't have money to buy maize. My family is in that situation right now. That's how women suffer.

Many weavers are part of the EZLN support base and they are the worst off.

- The women supporting the Zapatista uprising don't have money to buy soap, salt or anything, they really are badly off. The organised women have many needs, some don't have maize or clothes. And they suffer even more because they don't have time to look for a little money. The thing is they have to support those who are suffering in the EZLN, send a little maize and beans, some sugar for those who are away from home. However, they don't know where to find money to support the rest and suffer for that too.

The Zapatista men and women never accept either official help or the food bags from the army.

- Now they don't even ask the government for anything, they always did before and were given nothing, so they don't now.

Despite the terrible hardships Lorenza says no one will give in.

- The women want to go on fighting, they will go on until the government complies with the indigenous people's requests.

The women from Venustiano Carranza and the struggle for land

In Venustiano Carranza the struggle for land goes back a long way. The collective memory of the indigenous women is one of poverty, work and the community trying to get land for crops. The population is made up of hundreds of *campesinos'* wives. They stay with the children while the men occupy a plot, then they take them *pozol* and toasted *tortillas.*

The women in the People's House of Venustiano Carranza, a mainly Tzotzil municipality, have formed a craftswomen's co-operative and one of their projects is a shop to sell their textiles and embroideries. Their cheerfully-decorated skirts and blouses are considered the prettiest and most varied in Chiapas. Upon entering the People's House, the first thing that attracts one's attention is an enormous mural of Emiliano Zapata. On the walls the great Latin American heroes are portrayed: Che, Sandino, Martí... with a little explanation of their heroic deeds.

Once inside the visitor is moved by an altar of flowers and candles and a row of framed pictures of men. They are the dead from Venustiano Carranza; the pound of flesh paid, yet nothing has changed. Many more have died without their pictures ever having been taken.

March 1995. The People's House resounds with lamentations. Some men took us to see the cause of the problem: derelict land the *campesinos* were claiming. The Ministry of Justice police came and shots were fired. Two died. At the wake in a humble house, several crying women sat by the deceased in his flower-strewn coffin. His widow caressed his face. She was crying out loud, as if saying a litany. As we were leaving for our car some men approached us and told us to go and see the other dead man. 'You can't leave, you have to go there too, for his family and his widow.' They wanted us to witness the dead, so that their deaths were not in vain, so at least someone would see them. We did. Another poor hut; the men and the children outside, inside an inconsolable young woman beside a coffin covered in flowers. Other women accompanied her, sitting in a circle. Both widows were left with families to feed.

This land is ours

There has been a decade-old split in the Emiliano Zapata Campesino Organisation (OCEZ), which runs the local council. On the one hand, there are the *campesinos* of the OCEZ-People's House and on the other, the ones of the OCEZ-CNPA (*Plan de Ayala National Co-ordinación*). The documentary film-maker Carlos Martínez made a video in mid-1994 in which women from Venustiano Carranza talk about the roots of their struggles, their problems and their day-to-day life. Thirty-five year-old María explained that the split wasn't good for anyone:

- It makes me sad because it brings more poverty and misery. We can't work well anymore and there are always arguments.

On behalf of the women of the People's House, a young woman speaks:

- We want a peaceful so our husbands can finally enjoy their work and not be looked down on at their work place; for our children to go to school without fearing that the army or the government will go after them or lock them up.

Another young woman from Carranza continues:

- We want peace in Chiapas and in all the communities that have suffered government repression, we are tired of being frightened.

A middle-aged woman adds: 'we want to see our children grow up'. Martínez asks her about her descendants: 'I have ten, but only six are alive. Two have left and four are still with me'. It is interesting that she claims to have ten children i.e. the dead are still counted. Those who haven't left the family home are 'still with me', the others live 'away from me'.

At the moment, women work collectively in their weaver's co-operative:

- We have an assembly each week. We do the work and sell it, we buy more thread, it is all a lot of work. Our mothers and grandmothers taught us to work. We teach our daughters and when we die our daughters continue.

An old lady explains: 'when our mother thinks we're old enough she teaches us, 'you'll have your little piece of cloth' she says, and if we don't learn she slaps our hands. With lots of work we learn to do the drawings and everything. We were raised working hard, our growing-up was full of hardship'.

Teresa tells how she learnt the trade:

- It's not so much destiny but necessity that leads us to learn. I was little when my mother died. I didn't even have my own clothes, I couldn't have any because I didn't know how to make them. Need made me react and so I learnt to weave by memory.

A thirty-year old Tzotzil woman unloads her pent-up anger. Her story shows the role of women in land occupations.

- We have always suffered, because of the government, because of the rich too, because it will always be difficult for the poor to get a piece of land, a struggle, a movement... So, both *compañeros* and *compañeras* endure the same things, because when our husbands go to take over a plot of land, we suffer as well.

- We don't mind leaving our children with just *pozol* and beans, so that we can be in the struggle too, waiting to see whether the *compañeros* will come back or how they will fare. Our husbands send for their provisions; *pozol* is what we send them because we are poor.

She talks about poverty:

- For example, we harvest maize and beans, and the amount we get isn't worth it. Instead of going up, the price goes down. When it's harvest time we have to pay off our debts. The money our husbands have left afterwards isn't enough to buy a pair of sandals.

For the children the struggle for land is part of their everyday reality too. A woman explains:

- The children see how much we suffer. My children say 'do you think I can go to the community or are we going to the struggle?' 'Yes, mama, we have to follow what our papa is doing.' And I tell them: 'I will go, my children, but only if you are all right even when there won't be anyone to look after you.' They say: 'Well, don't worry about that mama, just leave us some *pozol* and then go. Whether you come back tonight or stay there, we'll stay at home. But when we grow older we'll do what our papa is doing.'

It is not easy to teach children the right behaviour.

- We teach them that the way our parents taught us is the right way. Never to be fooled by someone who says 'we'll pay you a hundred thousand or two hundred thousand pesos to come with us'. We don't let ourselves be fooled. That's what we are teaching our children, that where the community is, we poor and our *compañeros*, Indians, as it's said we are, that's where we must be. Because I think

135

division is the idea of the rich people or the government. We can see that if they're government people they don't lack anything, whether they work or not, they have enough food. But when we don't let ourselves be fooled, if we work, we'll eat, if not, there won't be any food, because we aren't government people.

Marta, another older woman, explains how she experienced the *campesino* struggles when she was little and that during her grandparents' time...

- There was already a struggle, but there wasn't a house like the one we're in now, together. Our parents held their meetings anywhere, they went out after breakfast and came back in the afternoon. Then they told our mothers what they'd been informed of or heard in the assembly. If we were adventurous boys and girls and knew there was a meeting, we went to spy and see what they're doing. Then we asked our father and he said: 'well, that group is a *compañeros* organisation...' And we grew up knowing what an organisation is. Once grown-up or married, if our husbands are from the community, we have more reason to follow them.

Teresa talks about her childhood and how the men managed to open the People's House, a centre for meeting and organisation:

- My father has been a community man as long as I remember and he's been involved all the time, since they began having meetings like that, out in the open or in rented houses. They made a huge effort to buy this plot and only with co-operation could they build the People's House. So we meet here to be together and figure out how to make our lives better.

The thing the women from Carranza would like most is for their children to study and learn a trade. Teresa says:

- We would like our children to study, but they are undernourished. We look at the rich people's children, who have a balanced diet. We are barely able to give our children some fried eggs, but we don't have enough food for them to study. That's why they don't pass at the end of the year. Why? Because they lack nourishment. Because what we earn isn't enough.

136

Chapter 7

Tzeltal women in the forest

Nineteen ninety-five was well advanced when we arrived at the Prado Pacayal *ejido* one night. As they have no electricity, a light bulb and a radio-cassette recorder were running off a petrol generator. The whole village was gathered at the basketball court and some young couples danced to the rhythm of a *cumbia*. It was Mother's Day and the whole forest was celebrating.

Actually the mothers weren't really involved; they were all sitting along the side, not dancing, because tradition dictates married women don't dance. Their children, as always, asleep at the breast or sprawled on plastic sheets or shawls on the floor. The younger ones were out to have a good time, in their best dresses, their hair adorned with colourful bows or shiny hair clips: barefoot, slender, and very young.

Images of the forest, images of the Tzeltal gully where women don't understand a word of Spanish. What a contrast between these Tzeltal girls and the girls in Guadalupe Tepeyac.

Government legal agencies do not regulate marriage or legal problems in El Prado or Guadalupe or Morelia or many other villages. Autonomy is a consequence of absolute neglect.

Shortly after the Mothers' Day dance, the representative of Prado Pacayal told Jesús and I how conflicts are solved in the community: an assembly is called and arguments are aired. For example, if a young man 'steals' a young girl with her consent but not her parents', both youths go to jail. The jail is a small cell with a tiny wooden grille in the door. They spend twenty-four or forty-eight hours there. However in the case where the young boy has asked his beloved's parents' permission to marry her and they refuse, then the fugitives won't be punished, but the parents will be locked up for not respecting their children's wishes.

137

- That happened recently; a boy had asked for a girl and her parents wouldn't even receive him, they wouldn't give him a chair to sit on, they shooed him away. He tried several times with no luck.

In the assembly where this case was judged, the boy's father was called as a witness also. Several times he had accompanied his son to ask for the girl, but they treated them with disdain and refused to invite them in. Since the couple were in love, they finally decided to run away without her parents' consent.

The whole village became a tribunal and, in tune with the revolutionary law on women, it was decided to lock her parents up and acknowledge the couple's marriage. With the in-laws behind bars, the union was celebrated.

Morelia is in the Altamirano gully. They too are Tzeltals and their traditions similar, explains Regina. She talks about what happens to widows.

- There are communities where everyone supports these compañeras because otherwise how do they feed their children? They give her some maize and beans, as much as possible. She can stay on her own as long as she wants to; but she has the right to marry if both of them are free. What we don't agree with is a widowed *compañera* getting together with a married man, because that upsets the man's wife. This person is punished, in fact both of them are. In a case we had in here, what they did was to send the woman to fetch stones and the man to burn fields.

Regina talks about how mistreatment cases are solved in Morelia, which as a Zapatista *ejido* operates totally outside the municipal authorities.

- If a woman says she is being battered, her husband will go to jail. Many women denounce it. Men beat them when they're drunk, if they're sober they don't, unless there are problems between them, like if he's with another woman, and then he has to go to jail.

Mar a tells of her double struggle

María dresses beautifully, like all the Tzeltal women of Agua Azul. Her white blouse is embroidered with flowers and lace around the wide neck. Her long blue denim skirt has multicoloured horizontal stripes. Her black hair is braided and she wears a red flower in it. María is thirty-five years old and unwed. Lying in a hammock in the schoolroom she says:

- We want women to get organised, to meet together, to learn to participate in the community, in the church and in different organisations. We don't want them to sit silent with their arms crossed.

After several years of struggle María says bitterly:

- People are always criticising me and my *compañera*, saying we don't do our work well and that we set a bad example. Since we left our community they make fun of us saying that we go out with men, that we hug and kiss in the streets of Ocosingo.

These prejudices are more rooted in the men according to María:

- Which is why they don't allow their daughters or their wife to go out. They think they are looking for another husband, that's what people say in the community.

María has to suffer the men's anger:

- They say we are on the other side, that we are not with the organisation which is not true. We are sick of putting up with everything, we want a end to all this suffering; and let them see if they can find other *compañeras* like us! We put up with their criticism and tittle-tattle. It's time they decided what they think instead of prattling about us. If people care to believe what they say then look for someone else; we've had enough.

María speaks sadly. I ask her about how she got involved in politics and in a flash I understand the difference between theory and practice. The left-wing indigenous decide in theory that women should participate and be organised but when they do, like María, all the men are opposed and won't accept her development. What happened to her is a good example: she is criticised now but at the beginning she didn't want to change. It was the community who nominated her to organise the women.

139

- The assembly nominated another woman and me. We said we would not be able to do it, we wouldn't know what to do, we were afraid. Just to think of speaking in a public meeting makes us nervous. Gradually however, as we began to participate we were less afraid. It was very hard to start with. If we get involved in the struggle then we no longer feel shame. At the start we couldn't speak Spanish well and we were ashamed in case we didn't speak right.

Lupe interrupts to tell her story:

- My husband lets me go out if I want but I feel ashamed to, so I stay at home. Except another part of me wants to go out. If we let our shame rule us then we will never get anywhere. We have to fight it bit by bit.

María continues:

- We've seen that the *compañeras* who go to a meeting or a course for the first time are very embarrassed, they cover their mouths with their hands, because we can't speak Spanish very well, because we are embarrassed and afraid.

Not all women develop like María. Often they taste freedom but rush back to their prison.

- In my community there is a *compañera* who was nominated to do a course at Don Bosco. She accepted and went but didn't feel good about it so returned. She was thinking about the chickens and pigs at home which is the most important thing for her. She felt bad in the city because she was worried about her animals dying.

- I always go out, and people say to my mother 'how is María, why is she always going out?' and my mother replies 'she has no chickens or pigs to care for, that's what we parents are for, we look after them'. They ask her how I get my clothes since I don't sell chickens or pigs. People are always criticising me because I am always out and about; sometimes the parish calls me, or I am sent to another state 'to see what they are doing'. Sometimes I have to walk through mud or rain but it doesn't stop me.

- People think I must be getting loads of money, that I am with the government, how else could I live like this. I usually go on ten to fifteen day-trips but I am always back for the assemblies.

Given that she is not married, María's father has authority over

140

her. He supports her in what she has chosen to do.

- My father agrees with what I am doing. He never says 'don't go' he just says 'take care'. He knows that I go out with the sisters from the parish, sometimes with people we know. My father knows what we want, that there should be *compañeras* trained to teach other *compañeras*. My father gives me freedom and he advises me ' careful how you go, I don't want anything happening to you on the way.'

It was a whole chain of circumstances that led María to become a women's leader and to break out of the traditional female role.

- I first left the community because of illness and I stayed a year in Altamirano hospital. My father said I should stay there as we had no money to be coming and going. The sisters asked me if I had finished primary school and if I could read and write and I said 'a little'. So they said they were going to enter me for a nursing course. Then I returned to my community. Then my uncle was bitten by a snake and my father couldn't take me to Altamirano so I stayed at home. But then there was a meeting of all the catechists in the area and I entered a course and after two courses was made a catechist. But once again the community was against me; how could there be a female catechist!

- By this time we had been participating in ARIC (an indigenous campaigning organisation). They were saying that women should get organised and also preach the Word of God. They were looking for area co-ordinators and the assembly nominated me and another *compañera* to co-ordinate the Agua Azul area. The assembly was mostly of men, with only a few women. So we would go around meeting the women in each area. The women don't have regional meetings because the communities are very far apart. Area meetings are more convenient. There are three areas within the region and we went to speak with the *compañeras* to inform them about our work and that they also can go out of their houses. We began to encourage collective working, for example raising chickens or bread-making. We were looking for what we could do as women and how we could get involved with something in the community. When the ARIC delegates met we would present our report of whether the *compañeras* had met or not. In the regional assembly we agree what communities

141

we are going to visit and report back on and then off we go.

- We go alone, and of course we are afraid, something could happen to us along the way. Thank God nothing has happened so far. There are only two of us left ; we began as four. But the other two were fourteen-year olds and they were afraid. We have no car so we walk. If the place is very far off they come to meet us. Gradually our fear lessened. We started in 1991 and the next year we were covering the whole region. When the problems began in 1994 we could no longer go out because then we were afraid. Again the *compañeros* criticised us because we hadn't met with the *compañeras*.

María explains something that I later saw in different parts of the forest. When it comes to meetings or messages addressed to indigenous women, those in charge of transmitting the information are mostly men and they tend not to pay much attention; only if the message is transmitted by women can you be sure it will reach its final destination.

- In January 1995 we held several women's meetings, all over the area but very few *compañeras* attended. The people who spoke on the radio didn't put the information over very well. They thought it was a course for midwives: that's pretty much what those men said on the radio. But it was a women's encounter on the Gospel. Women from only two communities arrived.

Referring to the tensions and problems arising from the arrival of the army in the forest María thinks conciliation is important.

- It is crucial that we poor people unite, because right now there are problems between the poor, between brothers and everyone is criticising each other. One is against the government and the other isn't; we are always disagreeing. And some sell themselves for money. For example, the other organisation (the 'official ARIC'), which belongs to the PRI, receives money. People do these things because they are needy, they have no money and that is where the government can divide us. Everywhere we hear that strength lies in unity. It is very important that both men and women know what is happening and how to keep going.

The Altamarino ravine

Our second journey with the women's project: this time the courses on health and human rights were to be held simultaneously in the Altamirano ravine. One of the parish sisters warned: 'women won't come to your course'. We arrived in Belisario Domínguez without setbacks, late at night.

On the road, I noticed for the umpteenth time the presence of *mestizo* women in contrast to few *ladino* men: in Altamirano, the nuns, in Morelia, two girls in the peace camp and in the little hospital, the doctors.

By contrast, in the indigenous forest communities there were only men. Especially on the first night. A man received us, another two kept us company while we waited for an answer and another invited us to present the idea of the workshops to the *ejido* assembly.

They took us to a zinc-roofed house where all the village men were gathered. About fifty men were sitting on benches arranged like in a church, or leaning against the wall. In front of them sat the village authorities at a rustic wooden table. A candle was the only light. With its flickering flame we observed that group of rough country men, in their hats or caps, shirts or worn T-shirts, sandals or rubber boots.

They made us sit down on a bench next to the wall. We felt like they were going to try and convict us. We didn't understand a word of what they were saying in Tzeltal or Tojolabal. After a while, they said we could speak. The women from Conpaz made a very careful presentation of the issue, overwhelmed by the semidarkness.

On of them stood up and presented in detail their project for training female health promoters in the communities of the area.

- Thus women can learn to attend to female illnesses, also help their community, the children and work, with the help of a health promoter. You will be briefed on everything we will teach, because we will give you a written copy so you know what we're doing and can check if you agree.

There was a certain stir. The men were whispering amongst themselves. There were no smiles.

'Ahem', one of the course teachers cleared her throat and

143

commenced a professional presentation of the project for women's training in human rights.

- Because of the situation in the area since January 1994, we think it's important that women know about human rights. A woman should know what to do if she is on her own while her husband is in the maize field..... what to do if a robbery takes place in the community or if the army breaks in, how to draw up a report or a complaint... The course on health is for two women per community, who must be elected. Three or four can attend the human rights one, we're planning to start tomorrow.

When she finished speaking, discussion in the indigenous language began. Among their long phrases a word in Spanish such as 'equal' could be distinguished. They must have been saying that these women wanted everything to be equal for both sexes, which didn't please many of them... Once in a while 'human rights' could be heard as well. The commissioner for the *ejido* gave an example: 'like in the Bible, they're going to study how they are, where to look them up...' (That was our interpretation of what he was explaining).

Luckily, the village authorities said there wasn't any problem in holding the courses. So they agreed to call a women's assembly the next day to elect the attendees.

We sighed with relief, stood up and left respectfully; the assembly continued. Outside, the moon lit up the night.

My previous experience of indigenous hospitality, as a journalist, was different from this occasion. Now that I was accompanying the women's group we were barely offered some cold coffee and stale *tortillas*, and that despite the very cautious tone of the women who spoke in the *ejido* assembly, who had insisted that men must know the course content and approve everything taught.

On the next day we woke up with fresh spirits and hunger. Rather than waiting for a breakfast that would never come, two of the Conpaz women went to a local woman's kitchen and asked her for permission to use her firewood stove to fix some of the eggs they had brought with them. Elena, the lady, happened to be very charming. We had breakfast on the smoke-blackened table in her hut while she was crushing maize and making *tortilla*. She was about twenty-two years old and had four children. She told us she was taking contraceptive pills and felt more comfortable that way, because she was having children too frequently. Besides, her mother had died of pre-natal toxaemia according to the doctor's diagnosis and she was afraid the same could happen to her. She explained to us that they've reached an agreement in the community to use condoms, they called them 'rubbers'.

Elena was pleased to have us eating and talking with her in her house. She was laughing at us, because we would have to cross a river to where the course was to take place, she said:

- And if you fall in the river, a fish will eat you, the fish will be nice and fat and I'll grill it afterwards.

- And you señora, don't you know there's a women's meeting to talk about the courses today?

- Yes, I've heard that; but I have to make my *tortillas*.

All the women in the village were the same. First they made their *tortillas*, hundreds of them, and then, gradually they turned up at the meeting house. Any meeting with women round here means an endless number of children running around, crying, playing or being breast-fed.

'It's very lively', Elena commented. About forty women arrived. After listening to the proposal, a few spoke but most were silent.

- We don't dare, we have to talk to our husbands first. No one wants to work in that because we feel ashamed. Sometimes men say things if we go out and that puts us off.

The Conpaz women were putting a lot of effort into telling them that not only single women should attend the course. Married women also can. They don't have to be literate: illiterate ones can do it too. It's better if they can understand a little Spanish, but if not, they can get support from a translator. Excuses and pretexts were being shot down, but they insisted it wouldn't be well regarded by men, that they had to ask for permission...

The doctor explained that men had agreed with the project and accepted for it to go ahead, that it was the community's decision. She also insisted that if those who enrolled were supported by all the women in the assembly, then they have to commit to it and not talk badly of them nor allow other people to do so.

- Everyone here is going to support those women to do their job.

Many complained that their husbands didn't inform them properly of the meeting:

- What happens is that men don't want their women out of the house. When they agree on something they never tell us. They're like that.

Another one said:

- Our husbands explain to us about the meeting, but it doesn't stay in our heads.

When they speak, these women crook their elbows and open out their palms, as if to say: this is what it is like, there's nothing we can do about it.

They came to a conclusion.

- It's good for us to try and do what you're telling us, because the truth is there's no place for our children to go to work, we have to defend their rights. I think that human rights is like, well, we can't rape a man, so they should not rape us. We have been told what human rights are, but we don't remember very well.

The meeting went ahead, growing in confidence, with more women speaking. Some women seemed already seduced by the idea of learning new things. One said:

- I'm going to ask my father; but the problem is that there's a lot of work in the maize field and I have to help him.

Suddenly, a small hand called attention to a corner. Hidden in the doorway was Lupe, an unmarried sixteen year old, who said: 'I'll go'.

Lupe had her parents' permission and was ready to go with us wherever it was necessary on that very same day.

The assembly concluded with several agreements: those who wanted to participate would ask at home if they were allowed to and the course would begin on 20th June instead of the next day, so they would have time.

However, Lupe came with us to the place where the meeting was called for the next day, to inform them about the course. She ran to her house and came back dressed up, her hair brushed and decorated with a shiny hairband, and a clean colourful dress, undoubtedly her newest. She was carrying a small bag with her most essential items. Lupita was the only one who didn't find the long walk over rough terrain a problem. She seemed relaxed under that hellish midday sun.

When we arrived at our destination, we were happy to see that some women had prepared beans, *tortillas* and coffee. There we met those who had come to talk about the courses.

The majority of them came nominated by the women's assemblies of seven villages to receive the information: few came to actually begin a course. The courses were explained, how they would work and those who were in a hurry went back to their communities before dark. About twelve stayed to chat. One of the doctors told them about medical things, that both physical and mental illnesses, like depression, were going to be discussed in the workshops, 'because we know many indigenous women suffer from depression.'

Some of the husbands who accompanied them were sitting on the grass quite far away. They inched closer and seemed to be really interested, maybe jealous: they also wanted to learn. When we told the women what was happening in the dialogue in San Andrés, they seemed to be motivated by a woman Zapatista comandante being present. She was Trinidad, a mature indigenous Tojolabal woman who was going to present women's demands.

At that stage, the waiting husbands had joined the circle and were asking questions. The men had a thirst for learning and they never imagined that when some learning came along it was for their women.

Chapter 8

The Indigenous Clandestine Revolutionary Committee

Why is it necessary to kill or die? It's so that you, and through you the rest of the world can hear Ramona say such terrible things as indigenous women want a life. They want to study, want food, respect, justice, dignity.
Subcomandante Marcos, 20 February 1994

Ramona, the Tzotzil Comandante

Ramona became a popular figure when she was seen attending the peace negotiations in San Cristóbal Cathedral in the second month of the armed uprising. Wearing her *huipil,* embroidered with a beautiful intricate red design, thirty-year-old Ramona stood out for being an Indian woman, more commonly seen selling handicrafts to tourists. Her eyes shone with sweetness but determination behind her black balaclava.

Ramona became an icon of a woman warrior, even though her role is mainly political. Thus the Zapatista movement had as their top leader beside Marcos, this diminutive Tzotzil weaver, who barely speaks Spanish.

During the negotiations Ramona gave but one interview, to a group of four women reporters. No male reporter was interested in her. In fact, she required little publicity. An image says more than a thousand words: it was Ramona who was carrying the Mexican flag which Marcos unfolded before the press, in an act laden with symbolism, as the government delegate, Manuel Camacho Solís, grabbed one edge of the patriotic colours.

The indigenous women from Chiapas were proud. They recognised themselves in Ramona and she was in an armed organisation fighting for their rights. Months later, in a women's meeting in San Cristóbal, the indigenous women wrote down as one of their resolutions:

- It's so good Ramona is fighting! We believe she loves us, that's why she's leading us. She shows us the way forward and what we can do. She is a mature person, an adult.

Tzotzil, Tzeltal, Tojolabal and Chol women took to the streets with new energy and there was no demonstration without 'long live Comandante Ramona!' being shouted. The indigenous women came to the conclusion that 'when we get involved and have meetings our hearts feel strong; if there's no organisation, if there's no dialogue, our eyes feel closed.' The comandante was pleased to participate in the peace negotiations and assured the reporters that even if she doesn't speak Spanish very well yet, she is prepared to continue being involved in everything.

Javier, a member of the Clandestine Committee, translated her words from Tzotzil:

- I came to join the armed struggle after quite a lot of experience. I had to leave my village and look for a job because there wasn't anything to live on. When I arrived in the city, I began to realise that women's problems there are not the same as in the countryside. I realised that the way we're treated wasn't right and I became aware of the need for women to be organised, because we indigenous women aren't respected or taken into account. We can't go on our own to the city. As indigenous women we are despised and ignored.

The EZLN's top woman comandante, famous world-wide, says:

- ...the fact that women are taking up arms is very important, because it proves we are all for the same cause and that women want to change their situation. Even though many of them are not involved directly in the armed struggle they want to participate in their communities.

Ramona, translated somewhat economically by Javier, for she spoke for five minutes and he barely translated for sixty seconds, expressed her idea of life and death:

- I think it's better to die fighting than starving. If it is necessary, if the cause is just, if it is for the benefit of my people, I'm prepared

149

to die, because we haven't found another way to justice.

It was not easy for this Tzotzil woman to be accepted by the community. Finally, in a big assembly, women elected her to represent them in the Indigenous Clandestine Revolutionary Committee because of her work organising and defending the weavers. In her soft voice she recited a long list of demands. She said that craft-work is extremely undervalued and that the weavers want better market conditions for their work. 'We also ask for crèches and nurseries for the children. There's nothing like that in the communities. Children go straight to primary school when they are older and it will be a great help for women to be able to leave small children so that they can also develop. We ask for food for them too, for seeing the children die malnourished is what makes us women suffer the most. We want canteens and meals for the children.

Rebel Major Ana María, delegate to the negotiations with Ramona, completed her account of the women's demands.

- We fight for the same causes men do, it's everyone's struggle; but among the EZLN there are now special demands for women. They demand the right to education because in indigenous villages and communities there's nothing for women. I learnt to speak a little during the struggle, in the EZLN, but when I first came I was just like Ramona, only speaking Tzotzil. We want a special school for women, where they can better themselves, even if they're old and learn how to read and write. Also maternity hospitals, because now deliveries take place at home. They put the newborn on the floor, in the dust, and cut the umbilical cord with a machete, the very same machete the man uses for working in the fields. There is nothing to prevent the child getting ill and no proper care for the woman. We want gynaecologists (we don't even know what a gynaecologist is) and workshops and machines to ease our work.

Javier, the comandante who translates for Ramona, entered the conversation on his own behalf and explained the Zapatista view from a male perspective.

- The women began to help. In the past they were dominated but as they started to gain political consciousness they saw the need to be organised and we, the men, agreed to giving them the right to

150

participate. In the past they didn't have the right to participate and even less so in an assembly. But they made progress and ended up demanding the Law on Women.

Javier said that since women began to get organised everything has changed, men help a little bit more, they are more aware of women's suffering.

- It's to our shame that we didn't realise before. Many women get up at two or three in the morning to prepare the food and at dawn they go out with the men, but the men ride on horses while the women walk behind carrying the child. And on the way back they even carry the firewood. When they go to work, they work the same, either picking coffee or maize, sometimes women do more for they are more skilled. They go back home and women have to prepare the food. The man gives the orders and the poor woman is cuddling the crying baby, grinding the maize, sweeping the house and even if it is night already, going to wash the clothes because she hasn't had time to do it during the day.

Ramona becomes ill

The Tzotzil comandante was not seen in public for almost a year. On 8th of August 1994 after being applauded and acclaimed by thousands of women gathered at the National Democratic Convention in the Lacandon forest, Subcomandante Marcos announced she was seriously ill. A national and international network was set up to help Ramona. But nothing was known about her. It was not until 19th February 1995, days after the military offensive against the Zapatistas and the seizing of the Lacandon forest, that her message on video broke the silence and the isolation in which the army kept the EZLN in those moments of great tension.

Ramona appeared on the screen sat before a table, with a copy of the 18th January issue of *La Jornada*. Behind her there was a white sheet with the acronym EZLN. It was the living proof that she wasn't dead as some alarmist newspapers had published. A female voice declared: 'Press release from the Indigenous Clandestine Revolutionary Committee, General Command of the EZLN'. She spoke in Tzotzil and in Spanish again: '...from this place in the Lacandon forest. Ramona speaks.'

Physically weak, but confident, the Comandante began her speech:

- Ours is an indigenous movement. It started several years ago to tell the world that the *campesino* people in Chiapas are suffering hunger and illness. I am ill. I might die soon. Many children, women and men are also ill. There is a lot of illness amongst us, but no doctors, medicines or hospitals. We are hungry. Our diet is based on *tortillas* and salt. We eat beans if there are any. We barely know what milk and meat are. We lack many services that other Mexicans have. When we go out to work, we are exploited. The artisans are exploited in the market, the maids in the city and the women and men in the fields. In the beginning, we asked for democracy, justice and dignity. Now we also ask for peace. We are waiting for dialogue, that's why we want the army to go back to their headquarters, so that refugee children, women and men in the mountains may go back to their communities to work for a better future.

- Once again we ask the Mexican people not to forget us, not to leave us alone, to help us build the peace we all want. We also ask them to protect Tatic Samuel [Bishop Samuel Ruiz], who knows our suffering well, who has struggled so much for peace. I want all women to wake up and plant in their hearts the need to be organised. The Mexico we all dream of, with justice and freedom can't be built without your involvement. Democracy, justice and dignity. Long live the Zapatista Army for National Liberation!

With this message, Ramona got national and international action to stop the army from entering the rebel communities. It was February and Subcomandante Marcos was surrounded 'and running through the forest', as he himself will explain. Another woman, the insurgent Major Ana María, from Los Altos, escaped capture by the military and managed to send the media a hand-written press release:

- Mr. Zedillo, you think that killing indigenous people and other fighters from our country will finish Zapatismo: Mr. Zedillo, you want to wipe out the indigenous struggle because you consider it an obstacle to staying in power and enriching yourself at the cost of the blood of many Mexicans. But all this, Mr. Zedillo, will be recorded on some page of history [...] We want to know, Mr. Zedillo, if that is your last word. Until now we've been given the order to fall back to avoid conflict with your army; but we are ready for it, because we indigenous people have nothing to lose and are prepared to die if necessary. We aren't afraid of death for we have always been living dead. We have nothing but poverty, exploitation and no freedom, justice or democracy in our country. This is the truth that you, the rich, want to hide from Mexican people. We hope someday our people will have dignity and justice - with peace, but dignity and justice.

In fact, with Ramona's message and Ana María's press release, it might be said that in the February 1995 offensive, it was women who broke the stranglehold that was suffocating the EZLN.

The Comandante returns

Months later, Ramona used this same method to speak to the world. On 24 July 1995, the day before the beginning of the fifth session of peace negotiations in San Andrés, another video appeared in San Cristóbal de las Casas. Her voice was better and stronger. She appeared outdoors, surrounded by vegetation, on a sunny morning. Wearing her unmistakable red *huipil,* Ramona thanked the world for being concerned for her.

- For the last few months we've known that women from Mexico and many other countries have written and sent their support. They were worried about my health and asked for me to get medical attention. I have no words which suffice to thank all these gestures of love and solidarity. In our communities, little girls are malnourished and when they haven't even finished growing up, they're already mothers. Many women die giving birth, leaving many children as orphans. When an indigenous woman is thirty or forty years old, her body is careworn and often wracked with illness.

- I thank you for your support and for giving me the hope to stay alive and fighting. But now I also ask you to work in solidarity for my sisters, for indigenous women all over Mexico, for my sisters working in the fields, in houses in the city, being mistreated in many cases, for women who can't go back to their communities because of the army, for my indigenous sisters who have had to go to the city to sell or to beg and most of all for the women who are sick so they can get medical attention. Our struggle is for justice and democracy, for a country in which women, children and men do not live in poverty, with its attendant illness and death. For a country where the medical care requested for Ramona today, can be available to all women, children and men. For a country in which everything we ask for in the Revolutionary Law on Women will be available for everyone. This will only be possible if in Mexico, all Mexico, we achieve justice and democracy ...

- For thousands of women in our communities, life is very hard right now. The army destroyed food and seeds; took away tools, and now we can't even sow. We women will believe in peace only if government soldiers stop threatening us, we will only believe in the government's words of peace if its army is not pointing guns at our children's heads.

'Long live the Zapatista women! Long live Comandante Trini! Long live women who show solidarity! Long live the EZLN!'

Ramona, now recovered, disappeared again. She only had to take off her balaclava to become just another woman in Los Altos de Chiapas.

The comandantes and negotiations on women

In the dialogue for peace held in San Andrés Sacamchén de los Pobres (before the Zapatista occupation re-named it San Andrés Larraínzar) the comandantes presented women's demands, expressed by another remarkable woman, Comandante Trinidad. On 9th June 1995, Comandante David, co-ordinator of the EZLN delegation, said to the press that it was necessary to open negotiations on women's issues.

- Women, whether indigenous or not, are treated as inferior to men. We recognise that in Mexico most of us men are sexist, that women's problems are not taken seriously. We give them no place in history and no participation in society. We are very clear about that. It is worse for the indigenous women who are illiterate, with no right to speak either, no voice in their community and no place in public posts.

- That's why women's issues are an important part of our struggle. The government, however, does not want any discussion of women's issues. But if these issues are not included in the negotiations we can always ask Mexican women to protest until the *compañeras* across Mexico and other countries too raise their voice and ask for a space in which they feel they have the right to speak and do things.

After this calm Tzotzil man, whose gestures and voice signal a deep inner life, had spoken, Comandante Tacho, an energetic and fiery Tojolabal, took over. Angrily he said to the official delegates:

- We were told that there can't be discussions on Mexican women's issues, that they can be dealt with along the way in other parts of the discussions, that it isn't worth having an exclusive round table on women. They said 'well why not also have discussions on young people'; they were making fun of our proposal. 'Why not a table on children or old people?' We said: 'Yes that would be good too.'

- But we felt their attitude was a gross insult. Women in Mexico have had no place and certainly no public status, particularly not indigenous people. That's why we have to campaign for the rights and freedom they deserve. Women have a place in the Zapatista army, they have proved themselves, they can lead, that's why we want to deal with their issues in specific negotiations.

Comandante Trini addresses the women of the world

The second meeting in San Andrés was starting. The convoy arrived from Las Margaritas, the depths of the forest, and stopped in front of the *ejido* house, the venue for the peace talks. Descending from the International Red Cross van, Tacho received an ovation from everyone present. Then a woman appeared: Comandante Trinidad. She came out of the night of Altos de Chiapas, her face covered by a red scarf, her gaze calm yet inquisitive. She wore her grey-streaked

155

hair braided, and a simple flowered dress and trainers.

It was Trini's first time at the peace talks and she was the only woman in the two delegations. She had never imagined being face-to-face with government officials, surrounded by mediators from the National Mediation Commission and legislators from the Concord and Pacification Commission. That same night reporters approached her for a first interview. She looked tired and nervous. The comandante felt alone among 'all those men' in cold, misty San Andrés: she, a Tojolabal Indian from the tropical forest.

However her optimism came across on that first night:

- We think that the government has the will for peace because it is facing us directly, not writing letters but sending senior, knowledgeable men.

Trini soon stopped feeling embarrassed with these 'knowledgeable men' and lost any sense of inferiority. Although she can barely read and write, she ended up telling them a thing or two, criticising them and calling them 'heartless'.

She came with a specific mission. She was mandated by the women of her community to demand the soldiers' withdrawal from the villages occupied during the 9th February 1995 raid. Guadalupe Tepeyac, undoubtedly the capital of the free zone fell into enemy hands and all its inhabitants went into hiding in the mountains. However, for all her demands Trini was unable to 'budge the bloody government'. Trini told me:

- It hurts to live somewhere else rather than home, your own *ejido*. I've always told the government people, please, put your hands on your heart and tell us, why if the governor gave us land to work are you filling it with soldiers? I'm fifty-four years old, and to still live under army siege, no way.

- I am here to say that we indigenous women, accustomed to work the fields, fetch firewood, tend our vegetable gardens and bathe in the river can no longer go out, because our communities are overrun by the army. We can't go in one direction or the other. Our communities have been abandoned and the *compañeras* can't enter. With the army there we can't go to our plots because of the soldiers and we've already missed this agricultural cycle. That's why I'm here as a woman representing all Mexican and indigenous women. Hopefully I won't be the first and last, but each time more *compañeras* will come.

Trini is clear on how the conflict can be solved.

- People in the community say that if the government agrees to peace and takes the army out, then the Zapatista Army will be content. That's all. But first they have to solve the problems that gave rise to the movement.

However, after the Fourth Meeting in San Andrés and seeing the fruitlessness of her efforts, along with comandantes Tacho and David, Trini concluded that Guadalupe Tepeyac should stand as a 'monument to government betrayal'. Its streets and houses would remain empty while its inhabitants would build a new Guadalupe,

- A monument to Zapatista resistance and dignity, in the heart of the Lacandon forest.

Then the Comandante tackled the issue of a negotiating table for women. Wrapped in a hooded black cape she insisted:

- We want recognition for our struggle. We feel the problems of our children, but the government delegation does not and neither do these men here. They don't feel it because they haven't given birth, they have never been pregnant, but we mothers do feel it. That's why we want to have a dialogue on women's issues.

- We want women's liberation, so we can solve things for ourselves, because the government has never cared about us. They always humiliate us, they say we have never been able to think, 'they don't count', they say. But women do count, a lot. We must speak out and demand women's rights. If I can't speak properly, then can't I speak at all? Given that we came here to the negotiations, we'll jolly well say something and in front of everyone.

Trini, the mother and grandmother, overcame her fear and with raised fist, repeated time and again for the TV cameras, the tape recorders and the photographers:

- I'm here to represent all Mexican women, all indigenous women, all the women of the world.

Comandante Andrea, the Zapatista mother

Trinidad didn't have to soldier on alone. Comandante Andrea attended the dialogue for the first time on 7th June 1995. She was wearing a blue shawl, a light-blue wool sweater, a dark fabric skirt, sandals and a balaclava. The same age as Trini, fifty-four years old, Andrea is part of the 'Grandmother Comandante' generation in the EZLN, those respected women who have encouraged the involvement of entire villages. Andrea has five children; she gave birth to all of them with just a midwife in attendance. She doesn't understand Spanish; in Tzotzil her voice sounds pleasant and fluid.

- The first time we come here, to the dialogue, it's a bit scary.

With translation Andrea says:

- I've been in the struggle for fourteen years. Traditions have changed, now marriage is better than in the past. Now it is fine in our municipality, they think more. We women work with our hands, with the hoe and machete, we go to the maize fields, we look after the beans. But women feel heavy-hearted when the children fall ill and when we can't cure them. We can't do anything because there's no money. Often the men are drunk, they drink and beat us, then the suffering is terrible, really terrible. That's what I want to say.

- When I understood the struggle, I understood with my own ears, so did my husband, we both did. But most of all, I understood when we had meetings and I listened to the organisers. That's right, yes, I thought. Then I was chosen to say something in an assembly where I went with other *compañeras*. But I can't write a word!

Susana: from downtrodden maid to revolutionary

Comandante Susana appeared a month after Andrea. Quite tall and slim, Susana was dressed in the traditional Chamula way: black woollen skirt and shawl with dangling red pom-poms and a white blouse with embroidered trimmings. Her balaclava was as much a protection against shyness as anything else. As Tacho or David spoke of the progress of the negotiations she and Trinidad stood to their right and left beneath the historic porticoes of San Andrés. Behind them the other seven male comandantes waited.

She was terribly nervous when we came to interview her. She bent her black head towards Comandante Trini's; we found out she was asking her how the interview thing is done, and what she was supposed to say. Trini, by then a veteran, told her to be relaxed, that we were going to ask questions, she only had to answer, it was nothing to worry about.

- We want the *compañeras* to wake up and for people to listen to us women, because before the organisation came [the EZLN], we couldn't say anything, not even a word. Now, ever so slowly we women are acquiring consciousness and so later on we will be able to talk and see.

The way in which the comandantes organise women is very easy, she says.

- We have women's meetings, we meet to talk. Without these meetings we don't get anywhere, it's only by meeting together that we can begin to awaken. We talk about the problems we women have, our situation, our suffering and our life, that we are exploited and not respected. After that women come to support the struggle. After we women got organised, gradually we lost our fear, just like that, through talking.

Susana says she's been for 'a short time' in this job, five or six years.

- Besides the meetings, women do collective projects like breeding animals such as rabbits or hens and also planting vegetable gardens.

All of this work was prepared knowing the war was coming:

- Well, of course we knew. It helped us and still does a bit.

According to this Tzotzil comandante, who expresses herself very well in Spanish, men didn't put up any resistance:

- No, not that much. We were almost equal; within the organisation there is equality because you can't make any difference, everyone is together. It wasn't that hard with the men; they thought our struggle was right, although they said in the past it wasn't. They no longer speak badly of a girl if she becomes a rebel and now a girl can enrol as an insurgent and nothing is said; besides we are all the same, women and men.

159

To explain the roots of her rebellion, Susana tells of her life before knowing about the EZLN:

- I myself experienced exploitation. I worked in the city for a while, I went out to work when I was little. There's where I realised work is hard. I asked myself: Why am I working away from my community? Why am I suffering here, why am I not at home?

- When I worked as a maid I was very young and ignorant and I suffered a lot. Gradually I became aware of my situation, it was very difficult. I didn't know any Spanish and I only spoke Tzotzil. Once I went to work in Mexico City, and that was worse. My mistress was evil. She even hit me and I still bear the mark. She didn't pay me anything, not a cent, and I worked hard in that house, looking after her child. But I knew nothing, nobody told me how to do things and there was none of my family there, I was all alone. I was about thirteen or fourteen years old. It was very hard.

- After four and a half years I came back. That is when I began to find about the EZLN and I thought it was right, because I already knew what we were going through. That's why I understood everything more when I met the Zapatista Army for National Liberation, I felt more deeply inside. It isn't right that we are beaten and mistreated. So I didn't go to work anymore - instead I started getting women organised. I went to my community and started. I told my *compañeras* how we are mistreated working away from home. We have to get better organised and not go out to work in the cities, and be united as women, because if we are united we can also achieve something.

First I was organising women in my community and then in other communities in Los Altos.

Susana acknowledges she was one of the main promoters of the Revolutionary Law on Women:

- Yes I said it was better to have a law for women and I went organising from one community to another so that there would be a law. I participated in drafting it, it was quick, I don't remember very well, but it was quick. You see, all the women, my *compañeras*, realised that we are not respected, so we made a law so that we will be respected.

160

- It was a bit hard for me, because it was a very difficult task to gather each community's opinions. The walking was hard; I had to walk for ages because the communities are spaced out. I went with another *compañera*, because I couldn't go on my own, because the distances are pretty great. In each village we had an assembly to listen to the women's opinions. Then we put it all together and sat down with the *compañeros* to compile all the opinions.

The Comandante says that in the Zapatista communities 'the law is respected'. Of the men she says:

- They also think the law is a good thing, they can't say it doesn't work, they have to accept it.

For the indigenous women of the future, Susana wishes:

- ...that they be free, that they think for themselves, and be free, really free. They should be able to do what they want, whatever it is. If they want to go somewhere or study then they can. Before it wasn't possible at all. Even now I can't read or write because my father didn't let me go to school, he thought it was bad. He has changed now and all the families have. Their daughters now go to school and study.

The youngsters: Leticia, Hortensia and Mar a Luc a

In October 1995 three new women comandantes joined the peace negotiations alongside Trini. They were María Lucía, a twenty year-old Chol, of broad face and oriental features; young Tzeltal Leticia and Hortensia, a slender Tzotzil girl wearing a red *huipil* like Ramona.

The members of the Zapatista Clandestine Committee agreed to be interviewed but they wanted the questions to be written down. Hortensia and Leticia brought their notebooks and pens and diligently wrote down the questions which they answered straight away. First they talked about the transformations in the rebel communities:

- The change that has taken place in the family is in people's ideas, because before we joined the organisation we had different ideas; men did as they pleased. But now we think differently and we are realising how we live, because before we didn't even know that we were poor... Women work more than men. In the old days women even suffered violence. Now there are families who don't live like that because the men share the work. That's the change that has taken place in the community.

- We had no alternative because we began to realise the terrible situation of women. It wasn't enough for the *compañeros* to get organised, we had to do so too. We have made progress and we know we won't stop until we reach our goals and until we see we're respected as indigenous women. Today, both men and women realise the importance of our struggle and that it's important to be organised. Men, women and children understand how much they suffer and understand their condition.

- It is difficult to change people's minds in some villages. Who is to blame? This lousy government and the capitalist system has dominated us all and that's what has been crushing people and stopped them thinking, but we have woken now. Now not only the state of Chiapas knows we exist, but the whole nation and beyond.

When asked if it is difficult to be a Zapatista comandante, they answered:

- The people themselves elected us, that's why we accepted. We're prepared to fight, we're here to listen to the people and our job as comandantes is to consult with the people, organise, lead and explain how the process of our struggle is going. We work together with the men, have meetings, make our plan of work and how to carry out our struggle. We go to the communities when necessary and meet many people in several municipalities. There are so many of us.

- Each village gets organised and has its own representative. There are women leaders, who give lessons in politics. These women put in a lot of effort because they have no support and the government won't come to solve our problems, or provide advice. The villages know this, because they've seen it for five hundred and three years of resistance and the government has never solved anyone's problems until the people themselves rise up as they do now. They have awoken and found the EZLN which will help them fight. So we help women to organise and to look for better ways. We don't want anything to do with the government. If we go and ask for the

162

government's help they will try to cheat us and put other ideas in our heads and other things we don't want here anymore. We've made the effort to train, to illiterate teach women, who don't speak Spanish and we've looked for the way to support them so they can learn.

Questioned about their personal situation as Zapatista leaders, the young women replied:

- We have no fear or doubts about fighting. We know we'll succeed because we will get organised and because we are determined. We are prepared to go the whole way together with the people. When we go to negotiate, we face our enemy, the government people. We're not afraid because we are prepared, if we have to die we will, for dignity, so that others can live. We are not afraid. We have said since the first of January that we prefer to die fighting rather than because of cholera or dysentery. This is how we see our lives and we know we speak for thousands of women.

During the interview Trini let the younger ones speak and watched fascinated as they took notes, reading and writing with ease. Finishing, Trinidad moved to a new subject:

- The rest of Mexico can do the same. Women must start to get organised, so there will be an improvement, because if they don't get organised, how do they think they will ever have a happy life? Well, the idea we have is to join with any independent organisation, so we indigenous women won't be organising alone, because alone, I'm sure we won't manage it. We think it is important is to join with other independent organisations, because we don't belong to any party.

- I'm just going to say one more thing. In the cities, there are other *compañeras* who haven't got themselves well organised yet. What we say is they should unify their thoughts and ideas. If they are too divided we won't make progress; only united will we win our struggle.

163

Chapter 9

The dialogue on indigenous women

The path is already open

During the first phase of the negotiations on 'Indigenous Rights and Culture', from 18th to 23rd October 1995, six large working groups were set up simultaneously to deal with the issues of autonomy, political participation, justice, culture, access to media and indigenous women.

About forty guests and advisers from the government and the Zapatistas attended the working group on women. Mestizo intellectuals sat together with indigenous women from Chiapas and the rest of the country. Here the white women had to listen. This group met for longer and discussed the most. For the indigenous women, talking was an aim in itself, a revolution of tradition. They had to go over the origins of their sadness and string together the paths of neglect and pain to go deeper into suffering.

Comandantes Hortensia, Leticia, María Alicia and Trini, along with the government delegates, with whom they got along very well, presided over the table at all times and concluded:

- We found that there are many women willing to struggle with us. And they exposed their needs and their problems. Their demands are the same as ours. Women spoke of all their suffering. For the last five hundred years they have suffered rape, repression and all kinds of injustice.

Trini was satisfied:

- We were very pleased with the four days of discussions. We motivated the women to get more organised so they will learn that the path is already open.

The conclusions they drew up were far from representing the richness of the debate. However, they raised their key demands.

- We want a total change in the prevailing economic, political, social and cultural model.

A particularly important point was the right for women to own land, which is denied by indigenous practice and tradition. They also demanded that the reform of article 27 of the constitution under the Salinas administration be rescinded. This had converted land into a commercial item for trade instead of respecting the rights of communities to own it between them. They also asked for reform to the fourth article on traditions and practices and its regimentation of indigenous women's rights and compliance with Convention 169 of the International Labour Organization.

Of health and rape

Health is the matter of most immediate concern to indigenous women. The woman, the mother, is the heart of the family. She is in charge of looking after the children and her husband, boiling the water, washing the clothes, cleaning the house, cooking and caring for her family. Whenever women are asked what they hope for or their most urgent need, they say not getting ill and having good medical care for their children.

On 21st October, in the El Carmen Convention Centre in San Cristóbal, health issues were broached. The anger stored inside the Indian women spilled out, as did the tears of all present.

Juana María started:

- I am from San Pedro Chenalhó, where there's a health centre but no health care for us. There are no doctors or medicines. A doctor won't attend an indigenous woman if she has no money. 'Go and wash your feet because you are muddy', they tell us, because poor indigenous women walk barefoot. 'I can't see you, you filthy thing.'

María is a Tzotzil woman who dares to denounce the daily injustices that indigenous women face, for example, rape by doctors.

- Why does it happen? Because we are indigenous women and poor, we are raped in hospitals. Women die in the communities because we don't trust the hospitals, the doctors or nurses any more. They never bother with us, they walk all over us. If the government

165

wants to provide service for indigenous people, it should learn to respect us. We want translators for Tzotzil, Tzeltal, Tojolabal, Chol, Mam and any language in our communities, in our Mexico.

A collective catharsis took place in the small hall where the women sat talking. One after the other, the indigenous women revealed the injuries done to them. Verónica asks for health centres with specialists in all branches of medicine and that they should be indigenous people, and even better, women doctors. After a short silence, Sebastiana, a Tzotzil from Chamula, asks to speak. Her words send a cold shiver up the spine of her listeners.

Sebastiana

- I belong to the reproductive health team of the Women's Group of San Cristóbal and we think it's important to be able to share some of what the Chamula women have allowed us to know about health in their communities. During the time we've been working with them, in pregnancy, birth, post-partum, we see that the different types of violence are always related to women's illnesses. Beatings and neglect are in many cases the direct cause of illness. The most serious problem that prevents them from living a healthier life is the value the community gives to women, which neither acknowledges them nor allows them to acknowledge themselves as having their own will. Authoritarianism, insults, beatings, humiliations, are accepted by women because God says so. He made it like that and it has to be like that.

- It is important to know the names of the illnesses and the statistics as regards women. But what we want to talk about is a little of what they have told us about their health. They, like many women in Chiapas, and in fact across the country, suffer headaches, stomach-aches, pain in their legs and their hands, and their feet get swollen, their bodies ache, and so on. They explain to us that the disease always starts in the head and spreads downwards and this happens to them because of sadness or fright. They say the sadness is because women are born with their spirit in heaven and they can't think how to solve problems. When she works too much, she can't rest. When the man beats her and doesn't even give her money for soap, she thinks about her sadness and it grows, then her head aches. To stop the illness she has to light candles and to pray. She is afraid when the man drinks and beats her, he kicks her and throws her on the floor. Then, in order not to get ill, she has to go and see the *ilol* (the traditional healer) so he will light candles, pray, prepare flowers and kill a chicken.

- If the man is violent and evil, he won't give her money for the candle, that's even worse, because she has to manage somehow herself to get her candles. When she is seriously ill, they never tell her what she has; besides, she never sees the doctor, why? Because he sees her pee; we say it like that to avoid saying that he sees your vagina. She doesn't think of pregnancy, giving birth, post-partum as a risk to her own health or life. If the midwife is there its because the husband doesn't want his baby to fall on the floor. Men don't respect post-partum (the days without sexual relations) and soon after he wants to touch the woman, but she feels ashamed because she is sticky, her skirt is stained. Sometimes, the man tells her 'you stink'; not even at that stage does he respect her. She can do nothing, her voice is soundless, what can she do if the man says: 'I bought you to do this', or 'did you pay for the alcohol or soft drinks when I asked to marry you?'

- A woman can do nothing because that's the tradition, that's the way of life. If the baby comes before time, or aborts, it's because the baby didn't want to live; so abortion is not seen as a health risk, even though she is bleeding, she still has to go to the maize field, carry the firewood, make the *tortillas*. Abortion means something only when there are no male children, if there aren't enough boys then it means the woman is useless, that she can be exchanged for another who can produce sons, because men want to have boys, that's the tradition. In the community she only has her family's support, if it was them who sold her. If she leaves of her own will then nobody will help her even if she is dying. It is also very common that in desperate cases, beaten, wounded women will go to the municipal president or the municipal judge looking for help. Then they reply: 'Did we drink your drinks here, did we drink your soft drinks [from the dowry]?' That's the practice in the communities, that's women's life, with no rights; we've asked ourselves how can a woman think of health when the person doesn't even know her own face?

Sebastiana stops abruptly, she has spoken passionately, with serene anger, a mixture of hardness and defencelessness. Her eyes are wet, her beautiful Mayan face is darkened. Sebastiana drops her papers, stands up and looks at the other *compañeras* at the negotiating table. And attacks fiercely:

- When have we enjoyed sex? Never. Because you aren't ever taught to. And how sad that it isn't a practice in our communities, it's not the custom.

Silence reigns, women are still drying away their tears, all of them, the government people and the Zapatistas, guests, advisers, reporters.

III from hunger and neglect

Ofelia Medina, an actress, presented some facts and figures. In Mexico seventeen million people live in abject poverty with no right to health. Eighty-seven per cent of indigenous children suffer second grade under-nourishment. One hundred per cent of indigenous children over the age of ten are undernourished. Between sixty-five and seventy-nine percent of Indian children attending school show stunted growth.

- The current health system is just another business to benefit a few.

Ofelia uses the example of the Guadalupe Tepeyac hospital which took four years to build and millions of pesos.

- No one in the surrounding area was trained in health care. On 9th May last I saw a woman die in that hospital. She came on foot from La Realidad to Guadalupe Tepeyac, a five hour walk. Five days earlier she had given birth. She was carrying one of her small children and her mother-in-law the tiny new-born who weighed less than a kilo. She died in that hospital which is supposedly one of the largest in all Latin America. We are ill from hunger, poverty, destitution.

Petrona, another indigenous woman, gets the attention of the meeting:

- We want two health centres in each community with indigenous doctors, one for traditional, one for conventional medicine. And we want women to be cared for by indigenous doctors and nurses.

Isabel adds:

- There are communities with huge hospitals but the care is not what it should be, there is no medicine and the doctors are still in training, they aren't even doctors yet. If we just have the building and nothing else, and women and children keep dying, what use are these hospitals?

Sebastiana grabs the microphone and looking at the *compañeras* she says:

- I am going to speak about abortion which I believe should be legalised because many girls are raped within the family. These cases are unknown because they are kept quiet. Sometimes girls get pregnant by their brother or father but we never know. I speak from experience, from what I have heard from my community, indigenous women who say to me: 'do you know how to make your period come?' I think abortion should be legalised and the reasons why made known. I have heard from indigenous *compañeras* who don't know what to do about incestuous rape which ruins the health of the woman for the rest of her life.

The final resolutions did not include the agreement of the indigenous women to request legalisation of abortion. They decided it was better not to antagonise the church, so left it out.

Because of poverty and racism, indigenous women suffer inhumane, impersonal, aggressive treatment, with no right to an explanation. Going to the doctor has terrifying implications for them:

- Also in the hospital, when they take their clothes off, a translator needs to be present to explain to them why they have to take their clothes off and why they will be examined. It should not be that you go to the hospital just like that, you get there and 'OK, take your clothes off, I'm going to examine you now'. It's the same when you're pregnant: 'OK, take your clothes off'. Without explaining it's because your baby is about to be born. And I'm talking about my

169

own case. I had a girl and twelve hours later I was made to get up and go. I couldn't convince them I was weak until I fell over. And I speak Spanish and can look after myself.

Women's presence must not be a joke anymore

Roselia Jiménez Pérez, a thirty-three year-old Tojolabal Indian, was invited by the government to participate in the Indigenous Women's Culture and Rights discussions. From Comitán, Roselia is a primary school teacher and president of the Zoque Mayan Writers' Union, with premises in San Cristóbal.

- I thank the EZLN very much for having made this dialogue happen. I love Zapatista women dearly, I'm very happy and proud to be in front of them, because as comandante Trini, Tojolabal like me, says, the path is already open: they have worked on it and it's made of blood.

Her great concern is for things to change after this.

- The first thing I said when I arrived was: 'for women's dignity, for the dignity of the Indian peoples, for the blood shed in Mexico, please, women's presence mustn't be a joke anymore, there must be an answer, we must see progress now'. That's why I asked for resources for women, so we can organise in municipal, state and national meetings and come up with answers to our problems. I'm going to follow up the response, step by step, day by day. I don't want it to be a joke, that they bring us to sit here at this table just to use us as they always have.

Roselia, with deep anger and conviction, continues:

- I want to see women studying now and managing their resources, I want to see women participating now. And we want a declaration so that within the villages, the community, men accept that we women are going to speak now. Blood has been shed to make this happen, say the Zapatista comandantes; I acknowledge this great pain we have, because it's our family who died and we who opened this path...

As regards the debate in which both guests and advisers from the government and the EZLN have participated, Roselia makes a statement about the indigenous women.

- When they arrived on the first day they said: 'sorry, I don't speak Spanish, sorry, I can't express myself, sorry, I don't know if you can understand me...' I told them please stop saying you're sorry. We are still saying we're sorry for not speaking Spanish. I asked them and begged them to bury that, we don't have to say sorry to anyone. What I am asking for are regional funds to be created for women to manage. Education is basic. There should be student hostels in Tapachula, Tuxtla, San Cristóbal, wherever universities are, so women can go to study and have accommodation and financial support.

Indigenous culture

Roselia talks about her life:

- I'm the daughter of a Tojolabal from González de León, my mother is from Lomantán, I was born in Comitán; they never let me learn the language, they said it wasn't good, but they never stopped speaking it. There are four of us and fortunately two of us kept that great treasure of the Tojolabal language, and the other two don't speak it at all.

Roselia, who writes in Tojolabal and loves her indigenous roots, demands once and for all an end to the inferiority complex of the ancient Mexican cultures.

- I'm asking for the official recognition of indigenous tongues and for the introduction of our cultural values into the syllabus, because until now the poor kids have been taught about other people's culture. Here is where the undervaluing of the language starts and the discrimination and where the culture is lost. The teachers arrive and what can you do if they don't speak the same language? They create traumas in the children, frighten them and create an inferiority complex in them. Children have the right to study in their own language from the beginning.

- Here in Mexico racism and discrimination prevail. Imagine, to stay here in San Cristóbal, we made bookings with some hotels but when they found out Indians were coming they refused us and that makes me sad. It is definitely the fault of the government and those people who won't accept their roots, because whether they like it or not, we have the truest Mexican identity. I don't know why instead of learning an indigenous tongue properly they learn English first. All the government institutions, even though they don't give anything to indigenous people, give jobs to a lot of *mestizo* people, but before learning a regional or state dialect, they learn English first. I ask for official recognition of Indian languages and for them to be used in universities, colleges, secondary schools. That's the way to make different cultures appreciated.

- I don't know where Mexicans think their identity comes from, because it's not mainly from Spain. Fortunately we have our identity and we're defending it. These lands, before they belonged to those who live here, were our forefathers'. We've inherited their wisdom and we know they lived in a truly great society. I'm not ashamed, thank God, of being a Tojolabal. Although I am here for the government, we're struggling for our autonomy, which is no more than the right to live how we live, for our organisation, to be provided with what is rightfully ours, not to have our values crushed but to see them grow, so our children inherit a good future without discrimination and racism.

A double disadvantage

Roselia's personal history is not happy. When she was studying to become a teacher, her teacher tried to put her down a thousand times: 'You are only good for washing *mestizos*' floors'. Then she went on to lead the writers' organisation, and

- There were men who wouldn't accept it, that's the kind of mentality that has to change.

Roselia thinks *mestizas* shouldn't participate so much in the discussions:

- I appreciate the participation of the non-indigenous advisers, but I think it is important that indigenous women speak, because what we're analysing is indigenous women's culture and rights; that's why I would like it to come from the Indian women. We are the ones who prepare the fire and who eat *tortilla* with beans and chilli every day or just *tortilla* with salt. We are the ones who suffer because we can't talk. The problem is that indigenous and *mestizo* women are struggling for different rights. We have a double disadvantage compared to them. We need to break down those barriers: we can do it. There are women here who know about human rights, autonomy, many useful things.

For this Tojolabal woman life changed on the 1st January 1994:

- We are no longer the same. There was hope before but we lowered our faces; if an Indian dares speak, and this is true, then he's a dead Indian. But fortunately, since the armed uprising our people can feel proud. The women too. We are different. I think we were injected with the courage to speak out loud. The four masked women in here give us dignity. That mask represents hope. Dignity has been retrieved. Even when we have to force our way through, even to get into the hotel. Most Mexicans' hearts are blocks of stone. But there are also Mexicans who are with us, struggling for our cause, to change the painful reality in which we live, not just since yesterday, but for centuries. And at certain times our people have had to die for claiming their rights and wanting to live with dignity. We've lived through that stage now, that's good.

- And I tell the Zapatista sisters: 'sorry I didn't take up arms, for not having that courage...' But I'm with them, with my pen and mind. We're struggling for a new relationship between people, we want to stop living in servitude, in exploitation, we want to be equal, to live in peace but with dignity, justice and freedom.

Chapter 10

Our hearts are set free

'Our hearts are no longer the same and neither are our minds. My grandmother and my mother lived in silence and they only knew the colours of the Virgin of the Rosary's *huipil*. Today, my daughters still sleep on the floor, still starve and are ill, but the kind of peace we want is different, even if we have to walk a long way to get it. I could leave this land, but my heart and my mind are different, they're no longer silent,' says Pascuala, in *Indigenous Women of Chiapas*.

The 1st of January marked a rupture in Mexico and created a before and after in Chiapas. Indigenous women began to react, wanting to learn, to get together and participate. The first Women of Chiapas State Convention took place in August 1994 and managed to pull together about twenty-four organisations. For the second meeting in October 1994, there were a hundred organisations present. They faced many problems. But for the first time indigenous women became protagonists and were first in line in land and council office occupations, road-blocks and in every single march for peace, for the withdrawal of the army from the conflict zone, for civil resistance and in support of rebel governor Amado Avendaño and Bishop Samuel Ruiz.

The Women's State Convention decided to join Avendaño's administration and create a Women's Commission with a programme of work to improve daily living conditions: hygiene, sewers, electricity, gas, drinking water. The lack of resources, the low intensity war underway in the state, as well as the difficulties of working in an official sphere, spelt failure and the women dispersed back to their own organisations. While the struggle to gain space for women was going on in the assemblies, at the rebel government headquarters an indigenous woman was raped by men from the Race Improvement Group.

174

In February 1995, with the federal army offensive against the EZLN and its leaders, the women's work was halted again, or rather it went underground. Fear gripped the communities. Entire villages had to flee in an uncertain exodus. As months went by, some were able to return to their homes, some weren't. The inhabitants of Guadalupe Tepeyac were condemned not to return.

For many indigenous women the Zapatista uprising led them to analyse their own lives and try to define which traditions to keep and which rights to recover.

One single book is scarcely sufficient to compile the affronts, demands and analysis of indigenous women from 1994 to the present.

- If a woman is single, how can she not have land? Women don't have the right to land, but women have to eat. It's an ancient tradition; but what's the reason? Not all traditions are good! A 'Chopol' tradition is that girls are married young and so what if they go away crying. That tradition must not be respected. A 'Lek' tradition in my community is that when a woman is older she can decide if she wants to get married. That tradition must be respected. Women have the custom of being only with one man. That's a good custom and must be respected. Men have the custom to have two or three women, sometimes sisters, we don't like that custom, it is better if it isn't upheld.

- In the organisations, it's nearly always men who speak and decide everything. They speak in Spanish and many women can't understand them. We're left out. Our houses have earthen floors, walls of sticks and mud, water leaks through the roof and walls. We don't have running water in every house, there's one tap for the whole community. In other communities there's no water. There are neither latrines nor toilets. Some communities have electricity, but many don't. What we want is a house with three or four rooms, one for men, one for women, one for the parents, a place for our things, a place for the animals and a separate kitchen, and where the water won't leak in when it rains. We want water, electricity and at least latrines because there's no water. We want to know if the government is going to provide and when; if it's going to be free or on credit. We want them to fulfil the Constitution.

- Since we don't know how to take precautions, we have lots of children and can't give them what the Constitution promises. There's no help for us. Children have to work when they're still small. My little boy carries water from eight in the morning to six in the evening everyday, for three pesos per day. We want laws to punish the fathers who abandon their children and don't give them any financial support. We want support for the girls to go to school, and books in our language. We have to learn Spanish so that we don't feel ashamed. We want to learn to write novels and stories, to paint and draw and design clothes and play sports. And have a school for adults.

On the street, breaking the mould:
Zapatista women on the march

International Women's Day dawned cold and wet, but it was to be celebrated like never before, as a great act of liberation. It was about leaving the kitchen, house, community, region and taking to the streets, and many did so for the first time. They left their husband with the eldest children and set off to discover the city. Four thousand indigenous women took over San Cristóbal on 8 March 1996 from the remotest corners of rebel Chiapas. The Choles from the north, poor *campesinos* with their hunger and pain; the Tzeltal and Tzotzil from the cold green mountain escarpments of Los Altos, in their embroidered *huipiles* and wool *chujs;* the butterfly women of the forest, the Tojolabal and Tzeltal, with all the colours in the world on their backs, intense, proud colours, a challenge to the grey sobriety of the *ladino* dress.

What an affront! Crowds of cheerful Indians arrived to challenge the racism and silence of centuries, with deafening shouts and hurrahs. And to cap it all, their faces were hidden. Behind the balaclavas and bandannas the downtrodden, triply exploited: poor, Indian, women, were partying and on the march. They were out to have a look, to meet each other and challenge the world with their Zapatista cause. What did the wind, the cold, the long walk, feeling sick on the bus or the weight of the children on their backs matter?

Not one would miss this occasion. All together, if out of sync, they shouted:

- Women know what they are fighting for: a life worth living!

Some men were moving rapidly up and down the march as it tailed back; the local and regional Clandestine Committee stewards in charge of co-ordination and security. It was quite a surprise to see how many were shouldering the little ones. Of course, because it was women's day, the women were the focus of the cameras, they were leading the chanting, they were the protagonists. They burst into the city like a window shattering inwards in a thousand shards.

- We women will leave our walls to take Zeledón to the firing-squad wall!

Quite daunting, these young forest women, whose simple appearance belied the maturity acquired in the EZLN. They shouted:

- Our rifles are put away, but not for good!

They marched behind their banners proclaiming 'democracy, freedom, justice'. They had their slogans ready on bits of paper and clearly they had been practising in their assemblies because as soon as the chant was heard through the megaphone they all joined in. They waved their fists in the air, not the typical left-wing clenched fist held skywards, but a circular motion.

- Zapatista women, proud hearts in motion; watch out we will change the nation!!

One behind the other, delicately, almost floating on air, the feet of these women trod the streets of the city which so despises them. Some muddy up to the calf, mud which spoke volumes of the distance they had traversed. Others walked barefoot on worn, callused feet. Most wore those ubiquitous ten-peso coloured plastic sandals. In colour, the Indian women flaunt their poverty.

The women from Los Altos lead the way, fewer hidden faces but more children. The future of humanity perched on their backs. The leading banner reads 'Long Live the EZLN!' with which it is demonstrated that the indigenous women are the prime movers of the Zapatista National Liberation Front, the civic movement which the EZLN is calling for. Its existence is proved in this mass demonstration. The owner of a car dealership watched them file past, brow furrowed, saying:

- They don't know what they are doing, they are being led, they don't understand.

- Are they really being led? - I wonder out loud.

- What is happening is that the people of San Cristóbal cannot comprehend that indigenous people think, much less indigenous women - comments another journalist.

They have come of their own will. They will derive nothing more from being here than the thrill of participation, tiredness and quite possibly a nasty cold. Their placards speak of their concerns and also show that this event was not cobbled together but deliberately planned. The banners and placards have been inscribed with devotion and care, with hope. A huge sheet of a banner is emblazoned with a figure wearing traditional Tojolabal dress: broad skirt, scalloped blouse, barefoot, brandishing a rifle. The slogan is :

'We demand the immediate withdrawal of the armed forces of this evil government from our villages and regions. We demand women's rights to social and political participation in our country.'

The women are outdoing each other in creative chants:

- Zapatista women are the light but if necessary we will use might!

The rally starts in the Cathedral Square after the march has wound through the main streets. The women listen to the speeches, sitting on the ground, huddled together. From their rucksacks emerge *tamales* and *pozol*. They buy coffee from a street-vendor and rest. The speakers gather on the wooden steps of the stage. The Tzotzil women commence after a man from Los Altos ' Clandestine Committee has formally inaugurated the event.

- Sisters, we call for unity in this struggle. Let us join together and bring alive one single struggle against this terrible government. Let's all of us women who desire a better life raise the standard of women's dignity and fight together.

A pamphlet read:

This 8th of March in Chiapas is historically significant for the participation of women in many social struggles -

occupying land, in blockades, protests, marches and so on, for improved living conditions and democracy and against this lousy government, against poverty and hunger. We support the Zapatista women when they say 'enough is enough!' and we support their Revolutionary Law on Women.

The rally was a real marathon, like all the Zapatista demonstrations of bravery and strength. At 4pm the forest women left for the bus home to their communities, while the women from Los Altos returned to the mountains to continue celebrating in Aguascalientes de Oventik.

With their 'hearts emboldened' the indigenous women returned to their communities, to their kitchens. More confident than ever before that something has changed in Chiapas and the door to their liberation is open.

GLOSSARY

ARIC	Rural Collective Interest Association. Indigenous campaigning organisation, today divided into two organisations; 'official' and unofficial. Both have been accused by the Zapatistas of collaborating with the government.
Atole	Hot maize drink
Campesino	Peasant
Comadre / Compadre	Friend of female / male gender
Comal	Flat pan for cooking *tortillas*
Compañero/a, Compa	Comrade
Conpaz	Co-ordinating Committee of Non-Governmental Organisations for Peace.
Cumbia	Latin rhythm similar to salsa
Ejido	Land held collectively by peasant villagers
Finca	Large privately-owned landed estates
Huipil	Traditional clothing of Tojolabal women
Ladino	Person who does not belong to any indigenous culture
Mestizo/a	Literally mixed-race; i.e. mixed hispanic and indigenous. In this context used to

	signify a person who does not belong to any indigenous culture
Nixtamal	Maize dough
Posh	Home-made alcoholic drink
Pozol	Staple peasant food made from maize
PRI	Institutional Revolutionary Party: for 71 years Mexico's ruling state party
Rebozo	Traditional indigenous shawl
Tamal	Traditional food made from maize
Tortilla	Mexican staple: flat maize bread
Tuxtla Gutiérrez	Capital city of Chiapas State, 80 kilometres west from San Cristóbal de las Casas

FACTS AND FIGURES ABOUT CHIAPAS

• Area: 75,600 square kilometres, 3.8% of Mexico's land surface.

• Population: Chiapas, 4 million, about one third indigenous, belonging to nine ethnic groups, each with its own language: Tzotzil, Tzeltal, Tojaolabal, Chol, Mam, Zoque, Mixe, Kakchiquel and Lacandon. Mexico, 89.5 million.

• Chiapas is one of six of Mexico's 32 states with a high proportion of indigenous people.

• Illiteracy (of adults): Men - 37%, Women - 63%.

•Malnutrition: 66% of Chiapas population suffer from malnutrition, the highest level in Mexico. This rises to 80% in the area of 'Zapatista territory' known as Los Altos de Chiapas.

• Chiapas produces 55% of Mexico's hydroelectric energy, and 20% of Mexico's electricity.

• Seven out of 10 indigenous homes have no electricity, and nine out of 10 indigenous homes have no water.

• Chiapas produces 28% of Mexico's meat supply, but 90% of indigenous communities can rarely afford meat.

• Wages are three times lower than the national average. 20% of people have no income. 40% of farmers get $1.74 a day, half the minimum wage. 64,000 families, almost all of them Maya Indian, farm coffee which has lost 60% of its market value since 1990.

• Infant mortality (66 per 1,000) is double the national average. 66% of the population suffers from malnutrition, one of the highest causes of death. The average life span in 'Indian Mexico' is five years less than in 'non-Indian Mexico'.

• 60% of the population is under 20.

• 30-40% of women speak only their mother tongue and no Spanish. 60% are illiterate.

• Birth-rate: 4.6%, the highest in Mexico (average 3.2%). In the 'Zapatista territory' known as Las Cañadas, women have an average of 7 children.

• One third of adult deaths are due to curable infectious diseases. 66 of every 1,000 children die before the age of 5, double the national average.

182

FURTHER READING

Autonomedia Collective. *Zapatistas! Documents of the New Mexican Revolution.* New York: Autonomedia, 1994.

Barry, Tom. *Zapata's Revenge: Free Trade and the Farm Crisis in Mexico.* Boston: South End Press, 1996.

Collier, George. *Basta! Land and the Zapatista Rebellion in Chiapas.* Oakland, California: Food First Books, 1994.

Holloway, John and Pelaez, Eloina, ed. *Zapatista! Reinventing Revolution in Mexico.* London: Pluto Press, 1998.

Katzenberger, Elaine (ed). *First World, Ha! Ha! Ha!: the Zapatista Challenge.* San Francisco: City Lights, 1995.

Ross, John. *Rebellion from the Roots.* Monroe, Maine: Common Courage Press, 1995.

ZAPATISTA TIMELINE

1520s	Conquest of Chiapas.
1712	Tzeltal Rebellion: 6000 indigenous peasants rise up and declare they will kill all priests and Spaniards. Rebellion is crushed.
1910	Mexican Revolution begins against regime of Porfirio Diaz.
1914	Peasant armies of Zapata and Pancho Villa occupy Mexico City.
1915	Defeat of Villa by Constitutionalist armies of Carranza.
1917	Proclamation of new Constitution by victorious Constitutionalist forces at Queretaro. Constitution enshrines land reform.
1919	Murder of Zapata by Constitutionalist troops.
1934	Presidency of Lázaro Cardenas begins, escalating land reform dramatically.
1968	Massacre of hundreds of protesting students at Tlatelolco, Mexico City.
1982	Facing debt crisis, Mexico adopts neoliberal policies.
1983	Nucleus of EZLN enters mountains of Chiapas.
1988	PRI uses large-scale fraud to secure victory in July presidential elections.
1989	Collapse of coffee price.
1992	Reform of Article 27 of Constitution, ending land reform; large numbers of Chiapas peasants join the EZLN.
1994	
1 January	EZLN seizes San Cristóbal and four other cities.
12 January	Massive demonstration in Mexico City, President Salinas declares unilateral ceasefire.
21 February	Peace talks begin in San Cristóbal.
12 June	Zapatista base communities reject peace proposals.
6 August	National Democratic Convention organised by EZLN.

184

21 August	PRI wins presidential elections.
20 December	Collapse of peso precipitates economic crisis.

1995

February	Army moves into EZLN zones, mass demonstrations oppose this aggression.

1996

February	Signing of San Andres agreements on indigenous rights and culture.
June	Appearance of new guerrilla force in central Mexico, the Popular Revolutionary Army (EPR).
August	Government repudiates San Andres agreements; EZLN withdraws from talks.

1997

February	Comandante Ramona goes to Mexico City, addresses mass demonstrations.
1 May	Autonomous Municipality Tierra y Libertad, with its municipal seat in Amparo Agua Tinta, is dismantled in a police-military operation with overwhelming force, with the arrest of 53 people.
10 June	Eight civilians and two police officers die in a police-military operation to dismantle the San Juan de Libertad Autonomous Municipality, in El Bosque.
July	Severe electoral setbacks for PRI in National Congress and Mexico City elections.
20 July	EZLN release Fifth Declaration of the Selva Lacandona in which they identify three obstacles to ongoing dialogue: lack of mediation, the war against the Indian peoples and the failure of the government to carry out the San Andres Accords.
September	Founding Congress of Zapatista National Liberation Front (FZLN), EZLN's 'civil wing'.
25 September	Heavy rains and floods affect elections, which are suspended in some areas by the State Electoral Council.

4 October	PRI win elections for the municipal presidencies and state congress. Many irregularities on the part of the PRI are noted by observers and opposition parties.
20-22 November	Three thousand members of civic society participated in a meeting with the EZLN, at which preparations for the National Consultation on the COCOPA's indigenous rights and culture law were discussed. EZLN also met twice with the COCOPA.
22 December	Massacre of 44 indigenous people at Acteal, Chiapas, by government-trained paramilitaries.
1998 4 April	Federal Judicial Police detain former General Julio Cesar Santiago Diaz for his probable responsibility in the Acteal massacre.
1999 6 January	Six former officers of State Public Security, who have been implicated in the Acteal massacre, are sentenced to at least three years and nine months in prison for the crime of transporting high-calibre firearms.
24 February	The State Congress approves an 'amnesty law for the disarmament of civilian groups in Chiapas.' EZLN are excluded from the amnesty.
21 March	More than 2.8 million Mexican citizens participate in the national Zapatista consultation on 'Recognition of Indigenous Rights and the Ending of the War of Extermination', organised by the Zapatistas.
1-14 June	Significant increase in military and police incursions in Zapatista communities in Las

	Cañadas of Ocosingo, arbitrary detention of suspected Zapatistas, harassment by soldiers at military checkpoints and the installation of new army camps.
20 July	A judge sentences 20 alleged members of the group responsible for the Acteal massacre to 35 years in prison.
9 September	A federal judge sentences Alfredo Hernández Ruíz to 32 years in prison for his involvement in the Acteal massacre.
14 September	A further 24 people, including the former municipal president of Chenalhó, are sentenced to 35 years in prison implicated in the Acteal massacre bringing the total number of people found guilty to 55 (all of them indigenous).

2000

1 January	5,000 Indigenous women from los Altos de Chiapas meet in Aguascalientes de Oventik to celebrate the sixth anniversary of the armed Zapatista uprising.
14 January	A federal judge revokes 35 year prison sentence against 24 people found guilty of involvement in the Acteal massacre on 14 September 1999 for administrative reasons and orders the investigation to be redone.
2 February	Presumed PRD *campesinos* ambush a group affiliated to the PRI who were on their way to reclaim land in the Suchiapa municipality. Two PRI people are left dead and seven severely injured.
2 July	Vicente Fox of the PAN elected to the presidency of Mexico, ending 71 years of PRI rule.